FLEXIBLE DIETING COOKBOOK

MEGA BUNDLE – 5 Manuscripts in 1 – 200+ Recipes designed for a delicious and tasty Flexible

TABLE OF CONTENTS

Introduction

Flexible ing recipes for personal enjoyment but also for family enjoyment. You will love them for sure for how easy it is to prepare them.

ROAST RECIPES

ROASTED CUCUMBER

Serves: **3-4**

Prep Time: **10**   Minutes

Cook Time: **20**   Minutes

Total Time: **30**   Minutes

INGREDIENTS

- 2 lb. cucumber
- 2 tablespoons olive oil
- 1 tsp curry powder
- 1 tsp salt

DIRECTIONS

1. Preheat the oven to 400 F
2. Cut everything in half lengthwise
3. Toss everything with olive oil and place onto a prepared baking sheet
4. Roast for 18-20 minutes at 400 F or until golden brown
5. When ready remove from the oven and serve

ROASTED SQUASH

Serves: *3-4*
Prep Time: *10* Minutes

Cook Time: *20* Minutes

Total Time: *30* Minutes

INGREDIENTS

- 2 delicata squashes
- 2 tablespoons olive oil
- 1 tsp curry powder
- 1 tsp salt

DIRECTIONS

1. Preheat the oven to 400 F
2. Cut everything in half lengthwise
3. Toss everything with olive oil and place onto a prepared baking sheet
4. Roast for 18-20 minutes at 400 F or until golden brown
5. When ready remove from the oven and serve

ZUCCHINI SOUP

Serves: **4**

Prep Time: **10**   Minutes

Cook Time: **20**   Minutes

Total Time: **30**   Minutes

INGREDIENTS

- 1 tablespoon olive oil
- 1 lb. zucchini
- ¼ red onion
- ½ cup all-purpose flour
- ¼ tsp salt
- ¼ tsp pepper
- 1 can vegetable broth
- 1 cup heavy cream

DIRECTIONS

1. In a saucepan heat olive oil and sauté zucchini until tender
2. Add remaining ingredients to the saucepan and bring to a boil
3. When all the vegetables are tender transfer to a blender and blend until smooth
4. Pour soup into bowls, garnish with parsley and serve

CAULIFLOWER SOUP

Serves: **4**

Prep Time: **10** Minutes

Cook Time: **60** Minutes

Total Time: **70** Minutes

INGREDIENTS

- 1 head cauliflower
- 1 clove garlic
- 1 tsp sage
- ½ tsp black pepper
- 5 cups chicken stock
- 1 head garlic
- 1 tsp olive oil
- 1 cup onion
- 1 cup apple
- 1 tsp thyme
- 1 tsp rosemary
- 8 baguette slices

DIRECTIONS

1. Preheat oven to 325 F
2. Drizzle garlic head with olive oil and wrap in aluminum foil and roast for 25-30 minutes

3. Place baguette slices on a baking sheet and toast for 10-12 minutes

4. Squeeze the softened garlic cloves on the baguette slices

5. In a sauce pan add vegetables, spices, chicken stock and bring to boil

6. Reduce heat ad simmer for 20-30 minutes

7. With a blender, puree soup and garnish with garlic

8. Serve with baguette slices

CHICKEN STEW WITH MUSHROOMS

Serves: **4**

Prep Time: **10**   Minutes

Cook Time: **30**   Minutes

Total Time: **40**   Minutes

INGREDIENTS

- ½ cup onion
- 1 cup cooked chicken
- 1 cup no-salt chicken stock
- ¼ tablespoon seasoning
- ¼ tsp paprika
- ½ tsp garlic powder
- ¼ tsp black pepper
- 1 tablespoon cornstarch
- ¼ cup milk
- 1 clove garlic
- ¼ cup red pepper
- ¼ cup shitake mushrooms
- ¼ cup button mushrooms
- 1 cup kale
- 1 tablespoon olive oil

DIRECTIONS

1. Sauté the onions and garlic together in a skillet
2. Add onions and the rest of vegetables
3. Sauté until they are soft
4. Add chicken stock, spices, cooked chicken and dry spices
5. In another container mix milk and cornstarch
6. Add to stew and simmer
7. When ready serve with rice or noodles

CHILI THAI SAUCE

Serves: **4**

Prep Time: **10** Minutes

Cook Time: **10** Minutes

Total Time: **20** Minutes

INGREDIENTS

- 1 cup water
- 1 tsp pepper flakes
- 1 tsp ketchup
- 3 tsp cornstarch
- ¾ cup vinegar
- ¼ cup sugar
- 1 tsp ginger
- 1 tsp garlic
- 1 tsp garlic

DIRECTIONS

1. Boil water and vinegar
2. Add ginger, garlic, sugar, red pepper flakes and ketchup
3. Simmer for 5-10 minutes, add cornstarch and continue stirring, remove and serve

GRILLED BEAK STEAK

Serves: *4*

Prep Time: *10*   Minutes

Cook Time: *20*   Minutes

Total Time: *30*   Minutes

INGREDIENTS

- 2 tablespoons olive oil
- 1 onion
- 1 baguette
- ½ bunch arugula
- 1 tablespoon wine vinegar
- 3 cloves garlic
- ½ tsp hot pepper flakes
- 1 lb. beef

DIRECTIONS

1. Mix vinegar, oil, garlic and pepper flakes in a bag and set aside
2. Add meat to marinade and refrigerate overnight
3. Remove steak from bag and grill steak for 4-5 minutes per side
4. Fry onion in a skillet and toss with marinade
5. Slice steak and top with onions and arugula

Serves: **2**

Prep Time: **10**   Minutes

Cook Time: **10**   Minutes

Total Time: **20**   Minutes

INGREDIENTS

- 3 Panini buns
- 1 cup egg plant
- 1 cup cooked roast beef
- 2 tablespoons mayonnaise
- 1 tablespoon pesto sauce

DIRECTIONS

1. Slice buns in half
2. In a bowl mix pesto sauce and mayonnaise and spread on each bun
3. Top with vegetables and roast beef

TOFU STIR-FRY

Serves: *4*
Prep Time: *10*   Minutes

Cook Time: *10*   Minutes

Total Time: *20*   Minutes

INGREDIENTS

- 1 cup white rice
- 1 tablespoon hoisin sauce
- 1 tablespoon rice vinegar
- 1 tsp cornstarch
- 1 cloves garlic
- 1 jalapeno pepper
- ½ cup basil leaves
- 3 tablespoons canola oil
- 1 package tofu
- 1 eggplant
- 3 scallions

DIRECTIONS

1. Cook rice following the package instructions
2. In a skillet heat 1 tablespoon oil, add tofu and cook for 10-12 minutes
3. Transfer to a plate

4. Add vegetables and cook until tender, add sauce, toss and toss until thickened
5. Serve with basil and rice

Serves: 2

Prep Time: 10   Minutes

Cook Time: 15   Minutes

Total Time: 25   Minutes

INGREDIENTS

- 12 asparagus
- 1 lemon juice
- 1 tablespoon sesame oil
- 1 tsp sesame seeds

DIRECTIONS

1. In a bowl mix lemon juice, sesame oil and sesame seeds
2. Wrap in tinfoil and bake at 350 for 15 minutes or until tender
3. Remove and serve

BASIL PESTO WITH PASTA

Serves: **2**

Prep Time: **10**   Minutes

Cook Time: **20**   Minutes

Total Time: **30**   Minutes

INGREDIENTS

- 1/3 lb. pasta
- ½ cup Parmesan cheese
- ½ cup olive oil
- 1 cup basil
- 2 cloves garlic
- ½ cup pine nuts

DIRECTIONS

1. Cook pasta and set aside
2. In a bowl mix garlic, pine nuts and basil
3. Mix with Parmesan cheese and add oil
4. Serve over pasta

COUSCOUS SALAD

Serves: *1*
Prep Time: *10* Minutes

Cook Time: *10* Minutes

Total Time: *20* Minutes

INGREDIENTS

- 3 cup water
- ¼ tsp cumin
- 1 tablespoon honey
- 1 tsp lemon juice
- 1 green onion
- 1 carrot
- ¼ red pepper
- cilantro
- ½ tsp cinnamon
- 2 cups couscous
- 1 tsp olive oil

DIRECTIONS

1. Bring water boil add cumin, honey, cinnamon, add couscous and lemon juice
2. Cover and remove from heat
3. Add hers, olive oil, vegetables and serve

TOFU STICKS

Serves: **4**

Prep Time: **10** Minutes

Cook Time: **25** Minutes

Total Time: **35** Minutes

INGREDIENTS

- 1 tsp tamari sauce
- 1 tsp seasoning
- 1 cup tofu
- 1 tablespoon water
- ¼ cup cornflake crumbs

DIRECTIONS

1. In a bowl mix tamari with water
2. In another bowl mix cornflake and seasoning
3. Dip tofu into tamari sauce and then into seasoning
4. Place tofu slices on a baking sheet and bake at 325 for 15-18 minutes, remove and serve

Serves: **4**

Prep Time: **10**   Minutes

Cook Time: **25**   Minutes

Total Time: **35**   Minutes

INGREDIENTS
- 1 eggplant
- 1 cup cornmeal
- ¼ tsp oregano
- ¼ tsp garlic powder
- ¼ tsp paprika
- 1 tsp olive oil
- 1 egg

DIRECTIONS

1. Preheat oven to 375 F
2. In a bowl mix garlic powder, cornmeal, oregano and paprika
3. In a bowl beat the egg
4. Dip the eggplant fries in the beaten eggs and transfer to the cornmeal mixture
5. Place the eggplant fried on a baking sheet and bake for 20 minutes, remove and serve

PITA CHIPS

Serves: *4*

Prep Time: *10*   Minutes

Cook Time: *10*   Minutes

Total Time: *20*   Minutes

INGREDIENTS

- 2 pita rounds
- 2 tablespoons olive oil
- chili powder

DIRECTIONS

1. Cut each pita into 8 wedges
2. Brush with olive oil and sprinkle with chili powder
3. Bake at 325 F for 12 minutes or until crisp
4. Remove and serve

ROASTED RED PEPPER DIP

Serves: **2**
Prep Time: **10**   Minutes

Cook Time: **10**   Minutes

Total Time: **20**   Minutes

INGREDIENTS

- 1 cup roasted red peppers
- 1 tablespoon olive oil
- 1 tsp lemon juice
- 1 clove garlic
- 1 tsp cumin

DIRECTIONS

1. In a blender mix all ingredients and blend until smooth
2. Remove and serve with pita chips

GREEN PESTO PASTA

Serves: 2
Prep Time: 5   Minutes
Cook Time: 15   Minutes
Total Time: 20   Minutes

INGREDIENTS

- 4 oz. spaghetti
- 2 cups basil leaves
- 2 garlic cloves
- ¼ cup olive oil
- 2 tablespoons parmesan cheese
- ½ tsp black pepper

DIRECTIONS

1. Bring water to a boil and add pasta
2. In a blend add parmesan cheese, basil leaves, garlic and blend
3. Add olive oil, pepper and blend again
4. Pour pesto onto pasta and serve when ready

ROASTED FENNEL

Serves: *4*

Prep Time: *10*   Minutes

Cook Time: *30*   Minutes

Total Time: *40*   Minutes

INGREDIENTS

- 4 fennel bulbs
- 1 tablespoon olive oil
- 1 tsp salt

DIRECTIONS

1. Slice the fennel bulb lengthwise into thick slices
2. Drizzle with olive oil and salt
3. Place the fennel bulb into a baking dish
4. Bake at 375 F for 25-30 minutes
5. When ready remove from the oven and serve

SPICED CAULIFLOWER

Serves: **4**

Prep Time: **10**   Minutes

Cook Time: **30**   Minutes

Total Time: **40**   Minutes

INGREDIENTS

- 1 head cauliflower
- 2 tablespoons olive oil
- 1 tsp smoked paprika
- ¼ tsp cumin
- ¼ tsp coriander
- ¼ tsp salt
- ¼ tsp black pepper

DIRECTIONS

1. In a bowl toss the cauliflower with olive oil, paprika, cumin, coriander, salt and pepper
2. Spread the cauliflower on a baking sheet
3. Bake for 20 minutes at 400 F
4. When ready remove from the oven and serve

Serves: *1*
Prep Time: *10*   Minutes

Cook Time: *35*   Minutes

Total Time: *45*   Minutes

INGREDIENTS

- 1 butternut squash
- 2 shallots
- 2 tablespoons olive oil
- 1 tsp rosemary
- ½ tsp salt
- ¼ tsp black pepper

DIRECTIONS

1. In a bowl combine all ingredients together
2. Add the butternut squash in the mixture and let it marinate for 10-15 minutes
3. Bake for 20 minutes at 425 F
4. When ready remove from the oven and serve

FRIED CHICKEN

Serves: **4**

Prep Time: **10**   Minutes

Cook Time: **20**   Minutes

Total Time: **30**   Minutes

INGREDIENTS

- 2 chicken breasts
- ½ cup almond flour
- 1 tsp salt
- 1 tsp black pepper
- 2 eggs
- 1 cup bread crumbs
- ½ cup parmesan cheese

DIRECTIONS

1. In a bowl combine flour, salt and pepper
2. In another bowl beat eggs and add to the flour mixture
3. Cut chicken breasts into thin slices and dip into the flour mixture
4. In another bowl combine bread crumbs and parmesan cheese
5. Take the chicken slices and dip into bread crumbs mixture
6. Place the chicken in frying pan and cook until golden brown
7. When ready remove from the pan and serve

ROASTED CHICKEN

Serves: *4-6*
Prep Time: *10*   Minutes

Cook Time: *40*   Minutes

Total Time: *50*   Minutes

INGREDIENTS

- 1 whole chicken
- 1 celery
- 1 onion
- 4 cloves garlic
- 1 sprig of rosemary
- 1 bay leaf
- 1 tablespoon olive oil
- 1 tsp salt
- 1 tsp black pepper

DIRECTIONS

1. In a pot heat olive oil and sauté onion, garlic and celery
2. Add chicken, rosemary, bay leaf, salt, black pepper and cook for 4-5 minutes
3. Remove from the pot and transfer to the oven
4. Bake for 30-35 minutes at 325 F
5. When ready remove from the oven and serve

GLAZED SALMON

Serves: *1*

Prep Time: *10*   Minutes

Cook Time: *30*   Minutes

Total Time: *40*   Minutes

INGREDIENTS

- 1 salmon
- ¼ cup brown sugar
- 1 tablespoon lemon zest
- 1 tsp salt
- 1 tsp black pepper

DIRECTIONS

1. In a bowl combine sugar, lemon zest, salt and pepper
2. Spread the mixture over the salmon and rub with the mixture
3. Bake at 350 F for 20-25 minutes
4. When ready remove from the oven and serve

FISH TACOS

Serves: **8-12**

Prep Time: **10**   Minutes

Cook Time: **30**   Minutes

Total Time: **40**   Minutes

INGREDIENTS

- 1 cup bread crumbs
- ¼ cup parmesan cheese
- 1 cup almond flour
- 2 eggs
- 2 tablespoons almond milk
- 1 lb. cod fish
- Tortillas
- 1 tsp Salt

DIRECTIONS

1. In a bowl combine pepper, salt and flour
2. In another bowl whisk to eggs with milk
3. In another bowl combine bread crumbs with parmesan cheese
4. Cut the fish into thin strips and dip first into the flour mixture bowl, then egg mixture bowl and then into the bread crumbs mixture bowl
5. Fry for 5-6 minutes each fish strip or until golden brown

6. When ready transfer to a plate and serve

SIMPLE STEAK

Serves: **4-6**

Prep Time: **10**   Minutes

Cook Time: **20**   Minutes

Total Time: **30**   Minutes

INGREDIENTS

- 1 can celery soup
- 1 lb. cube steaks
- ¼ cup red onion
- 4 garlic cloves
- 1 stalk celery
- ¼ cup carrot
- 1 tsp cumin
- 1 tsp coriander
- salt

DIRECTIONS

1. In a pan heat olive oil and sauté onion, cloves, celery and carrot
2. In a bowl combine celery soup with sautéed vegetables
3. Brown the cube steaks and set aside
4. Pour the sautéed vegetables and mixture into a pan, add cube steaks and cook until vegetables are soft
5. When ready remove from heat and serve

CHEESE PESTO

Serves: **2**

Prep Time: **5**   Minutes

Cook Time: **5**   Minutes

Total Time: *10*   Minutes

INGREDIENTS

- 1 can spinach
- ¼ cup water
- ¼ cup cottage cheese
- ¼ cup basil
- 2 tablespoon parmesan cheese
- 1 tablespoon olive oil
- 3 cloves garlic
- 1 tsp black pepper

DIRECTIONS

1. Place all ingredients in a blender and blend until smooth
2. When ready serve with cooked pasta

ARUGULA SALAD

Serves: *1*
Prep Time: 5   Minutes

Cook Time: 5   Minutes

Total Time: *10*   Minutes

INGREDIENTS

- 2 cups arugula leaves
- ¼ cup cranberries
- ¼ cup honey
- ¼ cup pecans
- 1 cup salad dressing

DIRECTIONS

1. In a bowl combine all ingredients together and mix well
2. Serve with dressing

MASOOR SALAD

Serves: *1*

Prep Time: *5*   Minutes

Cook Time: *5*   Minutes

Total Time: *10*   Minutes

INGREDIENTS

- ¼ cup masoor
- ¼ cup cucumber
- ½ cup carrot
- ¼ cup tomatoes
- ¼ cup onion

SALAD DRESSING

- ¼ tablespoon olive oil
- 1 tsp lemon juice
- ¼ tsp green chillies

DIRECTIONS

1. In a bowl combine all ingredients together and mix well
2. Add salad dressing, toss well and serve

Serves: **4**

Prep Time: **10**   Minutes

Cook Time: **5**   Minutes

Total Time: **15**   Minutes

INGREDIENTS
Salad
- 3 tbs basil leaves
- 100g Kalamata olives
- 3 tbs pine nuts
- 2 green shallots
- ½ sun dried tomato
- 1 cup rice

Dressing
- 3 tbs oil
- Pepper
- 2 tbs mustard
- 3 tbs lemon juice
- Salt
- 1 clove garlic

DIRECTIONS

1. Cook the rice

2. Mix the dressing ingredients together
3. Mix the salad ingredients with the rice in a bowl
4. Add the dressing and serve

TUNA SALAD

Serves: *4*

Prep Time: *10*   Minutes

Cook Time: *30*   Minutes

Total Time: *40*   Minutes

INGREDIENTS

- 2 5OZ. can tuna
- 1/3 cup mayonnaise
- ¼ cup chopped Kalamata
- 2 tablespoons red onion
- 2 tablespoons red peppers
- 2 tablespoons basil
- 1 tablespoon capers
- 1 tablespoon lemon juice

DIRECTIONS

1. In a bowl combine all ingredients together and mix well
2. Serve when ready

SALMON SALAD

Serves: *2*

Prep Time: *10*   Minutes

Cook Time: *10*   Minutes

Total Time: *20*   Minutes

INGREDIENTS

- 2 salmon fillets
- 1 cup cucumber
- 1 red onion
- 1 tablespoon capers
- 1 tablespoon dill
- 1 tablespoon balsamic vinegar
- 1 tablespoon olive oil
- ¼ tsp pepper

DIRECTIONS

1. In a bowl add salmon, cucumber, capers, red onion and toss
2. In a jar add olive oil, vinegar and pour over salmon, toss again

SALAD WITH ROASTED STRAWBERRY DRESSING

Serves: **4**

Prep Time: **10**   Minutes

Cook Time: **50**   Minutes

Total Time: **60**   Minutes

INGREDIENTS

- 1 pint fresh strawberries
- 1 red apple
- 1 sweet potato
- 1 large onion
- 1 tablespoon coconut oil
- 1 chopped cabbage
- ½ cup tomatoes
- 1 tablespoon almonds
- 1 tablespoon basil
- 2 tsp orange zest
- 1 banana

DIRECTIONS

1. Preheat the oven to 375 F and place the strawberries on a baking sheet
2. On another baking sheet place, the potatoes and onions

3. Rub all the ingredients with with coconut oil and place them in the oven for 45-50 minutes

4. Remove from the oven and scoop out the sweet potato flesh

5. In a bowl mix tomato, almonds, cabbage, apple and basil

6. In a blender puree the roasted strawberries and banana pour over the salad mixture and toss to combine

Serves: **2**

Prep Time: **10**   Minutes

Cook Time: **10**   Minutes

Total Time: **20**   Minutes

INGREDIENTS

- 1 head cauliflower
- 1 tablespoon avocado oil
- 3 cups salad greens
- 1/3 cup red onion
- 1 pear
- harissa sauce
- 1 green bell
- 1 tablespoon parsley
- 1 tablespoon lemon zest
- 1 head Swiss chard
- 1 tomato

DIRECTIONS

1. Preheat oven to 375 F and place the cauliflower on a baking sheet and drizzle with oil and salt
2. Roast for 35-40 minutes and remove when ready

3. In a bowl mix pepper, onion, parsley, Swiss chard, tomato and the roasted cauliflower

4. In another bowl whisk the lemon juice with harissa sauce and drizzle the dressing over salad

GREEN BEAN SALAD

Serves: *2*
Prep Time: *10*   Minutes

Cook Time: *10*   Minutes

Total Time: *20*   Minutes

INGREDIENTS

- 2 lbs. green beans
- juice of 1 orange
- 1 tsp orange zest
- 2 carrots
- 1 apple
- 2 stalks celery

DIRECTIONS

1. Stem the beans in pot over medium heat for 5-6 minutes and remove when ready
2. Add the carrots to the bowl and the steamed greens beans, celery and apple
3. In another bowl mix pepper, salt, orange juice and drizzle over the salad mixture

STEW RECIPES

FISH STEW

Serves: **4**

Prep Time: **15** Minutes

Cook Time: **45** Minutes

Total Time: **60** Minutes

INGREDIENTS

- 1 fennel bulb
- 1 red onion
- 2 garlic cloves
- 2 tablespoons olive oil
- 1 cup white wine
- 1 tablespoon fennel seeds
- 4 bay leaves
- 2 cups chicken stock
- 8 oz. halibut
- 12 oz. haddock

DIRECTIONS

1. Chop all ingredients in big chunks

2. In a large pot heat olive oil and add ingredients one by one
3. Cook for 5-6 or until slightly brown
4. Add remaining ingredients and cook until tender, 35-45 minutes
5. Season while stirring on low heat
6. When ready remove from heat and serve

BUTTERNUT SQUASH STEW

Serves: *4*

Prep Time: *15* Minutes

Cook Time: *45* Minutes

Total Time: *60* Minutes

INGREDIENTS

- 2 tablespoons olive oil
- 2 red onions
- 2 cloves garlic
- 1. Tablespoon rosemary
- 1 tablespoon thyme
- 2 lb. beef
- 1 cup white wine
- 1 cup butternut squash
- 2 cups beef broth
- ½ cup tomatoes

DIRECTIONS

1. Chop all ingredients in big chunks
2. In a large pot heat olive oil and add ingredients one by one
3. Cook for 5-6 or until slightly brown
4. Add remaining ingredients and cook until tender, 35-45 minutes

5. Season while stirring on low heat
6. When ready remove from heat and serve

CASSEROLE RECIPES

BACON CASSEROLE

Serves: **4**

Prep Time: **10**   Minutes

Cook Time: **15**   Minutes

Total Time: **25**   Minutes

INGREDIENTS

- 4-5 slices bacon
- 3-4 tablespoons butter
- 5-6 tablespoons flour
- 2 cups milk
- 3 cups cheddar cheese
- 2 cups chicken breast
- 1 tsp seasoning mix

DIRECTIONS

1. Sauté the veggies and set aside
2. Preheat the oven to 425 F
3. Transfer the sautéed veggies to a baking dish, add remaining ingredients to the baking dish
4. Mix well, add seasoning and place the dish in the oven
5. Bake for 12-15 minutes or until slightly brown

6. When ready remove from the oven and serve

CHICKEN CASSEROLE

Serves: **4**

Prep Time: **10**   Minutes

Cook Time: **40**   Minutes

Total Time: **50**   Minutes

INGREDIENTS

- 1 cup Greek yogurt
- ½ cup grape juice
- 1 cup mushroom soup
- 1 cup cooked rice

DIRECTIONS

1. In a bowl add mushrooms, yogurt, grape juice and combine
2. Place the chicken breast in a prepare baking dish and pour the mixture over the chicken
3. Bake for 35-40 minutes at 325 F
4. When ready remove from the oven and serve with rice

ENCHILADA CASSEROLE

Serves: **4**

Prep Time: **10**   Minutes

Cook Time: **25**   Minutes

Total Time: **35**   Minutes

INGREDIENTS

-   1 tablespoon olive oil
-   1 red onion
-   1 bell pepper
-   2 cloves garlic
-   1 can black beans
-   1 cup chicken
-   1 can green chilis
-   1 can enchilada sauce
-   1 cup cheddar cheese
-   1 cup sour cream

DIRECTIONS

1. Sauté the veggies and set aside
2. Preheat the oven to 425 F
3. Transfer the sautéed veggies to a baking dish, add remaining ingredients to the baking dish
4. Mix well, add seasoning and place the dish in the oven

5. Bake for 15-25 minutes or until slightly brown
6. When ready remove from the oven and serve

CASSEROLE PIZZA

Serves: **6-8**
Prep Time: **10**   Minutes

Cook Time: **15**   Minutes

Total Time: **25**   Minutes

INGREDIENTS

- 1 pizza crust
- ½ cup tomato sauce
- ¼ black pepper
- 1 cup zucchini slices
- 1 cup mozzarella cheese
- 1 cup olives

DIRECTIONS

1. Spread tomato sauce on the pizza crust
2. Place all the toppings on the pizza crust
3. Bake the pizza at 425 F for 12-15 minutes
4. When ready remove pizza from the oven and serve

SECOND COOKBOOK

MUSHROOM OMELETTE

Serves: *1*

Prep Time: *5*   Minutes

Cook Time: *10*   Minutes

Total Time: *15*   Minutes

INGREDIENTS

- 2 eggs
- ¼ tsp salt
- ¼ tsp black pepper
- 1 tablespoon olive oil
- ¼ cup cheese
- ¼ tsp basil
- 1 cup mushrooms

DIRECTIONS

1. In a bowl combine all ingredients together and mix well
2. In a skillet heat olive oil and pour the egg mixture
3. Cook for 1-2 minutes per side
4. When ready remove omelette from the skillet and serve

SKINNY OMELETTE

Serves: 2
Prep Time: 10 Minutes

Cook Time: 10 Minutes

Total Time: 20 Minutes

INGREDIENTS

- 2 eggs
- pinch of salt
- 1 tablespoon chives
- 1 tablespoon pesto
- bit of goat cheese
- handful of salad greens

DIRECTIONS

1. In a bowl beat eggs and pour in a skillet over medium heat, sprinkle with chives, and spread the pesto across the omelette
2. Sprinkle salad greens, cheese and season with salt

VEGGIE QUINOA CUPS

Serves: **6**

Prep Time: **10** Minutes

Cook Time: **10** Minutes

Total Time: **20** Minutes

INGREDIENTS

- ½ cup quinoa
- 1 tablespoon olive oil
- 1 onion
- 3 cups spinach leaves
- 1 garlic clove
- ¼ shallot
- salt
- ¼ cup cheddar cheese
- ¼ cup parmesan cheese
- 1 egg

DIRECTIONS

1. Preheat oven to 350 F and line a six-cup muffin pan
2. Combine water and quinoa in a saucepan and bring to boil
3. Lower the heat and cook for 12-15 minutes, remove from heat and allow to cool
4. In a skillet heat oil, add onion and cook for 4-5 minutes

5. Stir in shallot, garlic and spinach and season with salt and pepper
6. Remove the pan from heat and mix with quinoa, pour in the eggs
7. Divide the batter into muffin cups and bake for 30-35 minutes

Serves: **4**

Prep Time: **10** Minutes

Cook Time: **10** Minutes

Total Time: **20** Minutes

INGREDIENTS

- **10 cups**
- **½ cup butter**
- **1 cup diced celery**
- **¼ cup onion**
- **1 cup chopped cranberries**
- **½ cup sugar**
- **1 tsp sage**
- **1 tsp rosemary**
- **1 tsp sage**
- **1 tsp rosemary**
- **1 tsp thyme**
- **½ cup parsley**
- **salt**
- **1 lb. ground sausage**
- **1 cup chicken broth**

DIRECTIONS

1. In a saucepan heat butter over medium heat, add onion, celery and cook, add cranberries, sage, sugar, rosemary, parsley, thyme
2. Season with salt and pepper
3. Brown the sausage in a skillet, drain off fat
4. Toss the ingredients in the bowl and add chicken broth
5. Serve when ready

CRUSTLESS QUICHE CUPS

Serves: **6**
Prep Time: **10**   Minutes

Cook Time: **10**   Minutes

Total Time: **20**   Minutes

INGREDIENTS

- 10 oz. chopped kale
- 2 eggs
- 2 egg whites
- ½ cup leek
- ½ cup chopped tomato
- ½ cup bell pepper

DIRECTIONS

1. Preheat oven to 325 F and line a muffin pan with paper liners
2. In a bowl leek, egg whites, tomatoes, kale, eggs and bell pepper
3. Divide mixture into muffin cups and bake for 15-20 minutes
4. Remove and serve

QUINOA WITH SCALLIONS

Serves: *6*

Prep Time: *10* Minutes

Cook Time: *10* Minutes

Total Time: *20* Minutes

INGREDIENTS

- 3 ears corn
- 1 tablespoon lemon zest
- 1 tablespoon lemon juice
- ½ cup butter
- 1 tablespoon honey
- ¼ tsp salt
- ½ tsp pepper
- 1 cup quinoa
- 3 scallions

DIRECTIONS

1. In a pot place the corn and fill the pan with water, bring to boil and cover for 5-6 minutes
2. Remove from pot and let it cool
3. In a bowl mix the rest of the ingredients for dressing: lemon juice, melted butter, lemon zest, honey, pepper

4. Cook the quinoa in a pot, add scallions in a bowl with the dressing and toss well
5. Season with salt and serve

BERRY GRANOLA

Serves: **4**

Prep Time: **10** Minutes

Cook Time: **10** Minutes

Total Time: **20** Minutes

INGREDIENTS

- **2 tablespoons chia**
- **¾ cup rolled oats**
- **1 cup vanilla cashewmilk**
- **½ cup fresh blueberries**
- **2 strawberries**
- **½ raspberries**
- **sprinkle of granola**

DIRECTIONS

1. **In a bowl mix cashewmilk, oats, chia and divide into 2 servings**
2. **Refrigerate overnight, remove top with berries and serve**

Serves: 2
Prep Time: 5   Minutes

Cook Time: 5   Minutes

Total Time: 10   Minutes

INGREDIENTS

- 2 tablespoons chia
- ¾ cup rolled oats
- 1 cup vanilla cashewmilk
- ¼ cup peach
- ¼ plum
- 3 basil leaves
- 1 tsp pumpkin seeds
- 1 tsp hemp seeds

DIRECTIONS

1. In a bowl mix cashewmilk, oats, chia and oats, divide into 2-3 servings
2. Refrigerate overnight
3. Remove and serve

AVOCADO BROWNIE

Serves: *4*

Prep Time: *10*   Minutes

Cook Time: *30*   Minutes

Total Time: *40*   Minutes

INGREDIENTS

- 1 ripe avocado
- 3 tablespoons melted butter
- 1 egg
- ¼ cup brown sugar
- ¼ maple syrup
- 1 tablespoon vanilla extract
- ¾ cup cocoa powder
- ½ tsp salt
- ½ cup gluten-free flour
- ¼ cup dark chocolate chips

DIRECTIONS

1. Preheat the oven to 325 F
2. In a bowl mash the avocado, brown sugar, maple syrup, vanilla, sugar, water, butter, add cocoa powder
3. In a bowl mix salt and flour and stir in avocado mixture, spread bake in the pan and bake for 35 minutes

4. Remove and cool before serving

Serves: *1*

Prep Time: *5*   Minutes

Cook Time: *5*   Minutes

Total Time: *10*   Minutes

INGREDIENTS

- 1 cup corn cereal
- 1 cup rice cereal
- ¼ cup cocoa cereal
- ¼ cup rice cakes

DIRECTIONS

1. In a bowl combine all ingredients together
2. Serve with milk

SAUSAGE BREAKFAST SANDWICH

Serves: **2**

Prep Time: **5**   Minutes

Cook Time: **15**   Minutes

Total Time: **20**   Minutes

INGREDIENTS

- ¼ cup egg substitute
- 1 muffin
- 1 turkey sausage patty
- 1 tablespoon cheddar cheese

DIRECTIONS

1. In a skillet pour egg and cook on low heat
2. Place turkey sausage patty in a pan and cook for 4-5 minutes per side
3. On a toasted muffin place the cooked egg, top with a sausage patty and cheddar cheese
4. Serve when ready

BREAKFAST GRANOLA

Serves: 2

Prep Time: 5   Minutes

Cook Time: 30   Minutes

Total Time: 35   Minutes

INGREDIENTS

- 1 tsp vanilla extract
- 1 tablespoon honey
- 1 lb. rolled oats
- 2 tablespoons sesame seeds
- ¼ lb. almonds
- ¼ lb. berries

DIRECTIONS

1. Preheat the oven to 325 F
2. Spread the granola onto a baking sheet
3. Bake for 12-15 minutes, remove and mix everything
4. Bake for another 12-15 minutes or until slightly brown
5. When ready remove from the oven and serve

RASPBERRY CRUMBLE

Serves: *4*

Prep Time: *10*   Minutes

Cook Time: *50*   Minutes

Total Time: *60*   Minutes

INGREDIENTS

- 2 eggs
- 1 cup raspberries
- 1 cup apple juice
- 1 cup oats
- 1 tablespoon butter
- 1 tablespoon brown sugar
- 1 tablespoon cinnamon
- ¼ tsp cloves

DIRECTIONS

1. Preheat oven to 375 F
2. In a bowl combine raspberries, apple slices and apple juice
3. In another bowl combine sugar, spices, oats, butter and mix well
4. Cover apple slices with crumble topping
5. Bake for 45-50 minutes
6. When ready remove and serve

QUINOA CREPES WITH APPLESAUCE

Serves: **4**

Prep Time: **10** Minutes

Cook Time: **30** Minutes

Total Time: **40** Minutes

INGREDIENTS

- 1 cup quinoa flour
- ½ cup tapioca flour
- 1 tsp baking soda
- 1 tsp cinnamon
- 1 cup water
- 2 tablespoons canola oil
- 2 cups organic apple sauce

DIRECTIONS

1. In a bowl combine quinoa flour, baking soda, cinnamon, tapioca flour, water, oil and whisk well
2. Preheat a skillet over medium heat and pour ¼ cup batter into skillet
3. Cook each crepe on low heat for 1-2 minutes per side
4. When ready remove and serve with apple sauce

CHEESE OMELETTE

Serves: *1*
Prep Time: *5*   Minutes

Cook Time: *10*   Minutes

Total Time: *15*   Minutes

INGREDIENTS

- **2 eggs**
- **¼ tsp salt**
- **¼ tsp black pepper**
- **1 tablespoon olive oil**
- **¼ cup cheese**
- **¼ tsp basil**
- **1 cup low-fat cheese**

DIRECTIONS

1. **In a bowl combine all ingredients together and mix well**
2. **In a skillet heat olive oil and pour the egg mixture**
3. **Cook for 1-2 minutes per side**
4. **When ready remove omelette from the skillet and serve**

CUCUMBER OMELETTE

Serves: *1*
Prep Time: *5*   Minutes

Cook Time: *10*   Minutes

Total Time: *15*   Minutes

INGREDIENTS

- **2 eggs**
- **¼ tsp salt**
- **¼ tsp black pepper**
- **1 tablespoon olive oil**
- **¼ cup cheese**
- **¼ tsp basil**
- **1 cup cucumber**

DIRECTIONS

1. **In a bowl combine all ingredients together and mix well**
2. **In a skillet heat olive oil and pour the egg mixture**
3. **Cook for 1-2 minutes per side**
4. **When ready remove omelette from the skillet and serve**

PANCAKES

BANANA PANCAKES

Serves: **4**

Prep Time: **10**   Minutes

Cook Time: **20**   Minutes

Total Time: **30**   Minutes

INGREDIENTS

- 1 cup whole wheat flour
- ¼ tsp baking soda
- ¼ tsp baking powder
- 1 cup mashed banana
- 2 eggs
- 1 cup milk

DIRECTIONS

1. In a bowl combine all ingredients together and mix well
2. In a skillet heat olive oil
3. Pour ¼ of the batter and cook each pancake for 1-2 minutes per side
4. When ready remove from heat and serve

BUCKWHEAT PANCAKES

Serves: **6**

Prep Time: **5**   Minutes

Cook Time: **10**   Minutes

Total Time: **15**   Minutes

INGREDIENTS

- **1 cup buckwheat flour**
- **1 tablespoon brown sugar**
- **¼ tsp salt**
- **1 tsp baking powder**
- **1 cup almond milk**
- **1 tablespoon canola oil**
- **2 bananas**

DIRECTIONS

1. **In a bowl combine dry ingredients**
2. **Add wet ingredients and mix well**
3. **In a skillet pour ¼ cup batter and cook for 1-2 minutes per side**
4. **When ready remove and serve with syrup**

COOKIES

MORNING COOKIES

Serves: **6**

Prep Time: **10**   Minutes

Cook Time: **15**   Minutes

Total Time: **25**   Minutes

INGREDIENTS

- **3 bananas**
- **¼ cup peanut butter**
- **¼ cup cocoa powder**
- **handful of salt**

DIRECTIONS

1. **Preheat oven to 325 F**
2. **In a bowl mix all ingredients**
3. **Form small cookies and place them onto a greased cookie sheet**
4. **Sprinkle with salt and bake for 12-15 minutes**
5. **Remove and serve**

BLUEBERRY BITES

Serves: *8*

Prep Time: *5*   Minutes

Cook Time: *30*   Minutes

Total Time: *35*   Minutes

INGREDIENTS

- **2 cups oats**
- **½ tsp cinnamon**
- **1 cup blueberries**
- **½ cup honey**
- **½ cup almond butter**
- **1 tsp vanilla**

DIRECTIONS

1. **Mix all of the ingredients together, except for the blueberries.**
2. **Fold in the blueberries and refrigerate for 30 minutes.**
3. **Form balls from the mixture and serve.**

GINGER LEMONADE

Serves: *8*
Prep Time: *5*   Minutes

Cook Time: *10*   Minutes

Total Time: *15*   Minutes

INGREDIENTS

- 1/3 cup honey
- 4 lemons juice
- Ice
- 4 strips of lemon peel
- 2 tbs ginger root
- 2 sprigs rosemary

DIRECTIONS

1. Mix the honey, ginger, lemon peel and 2 sprigs rosemary in a pot with 2 cups water.
2. Bring to a boil, then simmer for 10 minutes.
3. Remove from heat and allow to cool for 15 minutes.
4. Strain into a pitcher.
5. Discard the ginger and rosemary.
6. Add 6 cups of cold water and lemon juice to the pitcher.
7. Stir to combine and serve with ice.

LIME GRILLED CORN

Serves: *4*

Prep Time: *5*   Minutes

Cook Time: *15*   Minutes

Total Time: *20*   Minutes

INGREDIENTS

- **4 corns**
- **2 tbs mayonnaise**
- **Salt**
- **Pepper**
- **2 tbs lime juice**
- **¼ tsp chili powder**

DIRECTIONS

1. **Preheat the grill.**
2. **Cook the shucked corn onto the grill for 5 minutes.**
3. **Turn every few minutes until all sides are charred.**
4. **Mix the mayonnaise, chili powder, and lime juice in a bowl.**
5. **Season with salt and pepper and add lime juice and chili powder.**
6. **Serve coated with the mayonnaise mixture.**

APPLE CRUMBLE

Serves: *6*
Prep Time: *10*   Minutes

Cook Time: *30*   Minutes

Total Time: *40*   Minutes

INGREDIENTS

- 4 apples
- 2 tsp cinnamon
- 1 cup flour
- ½ cup walnuts
- 2 cups quinoa
- 1/3 cup ground almonds

DIRECTIONS

1. Preheat the oven to 350F.
2. Oil a baking dish.
3. Place the apples into prepared dishes.
4. Mix the remaining ingredients in a bowl.
5. Crumble over the apples.
6. Bake for 30 minutes.
7. Serve immediately.

Serves: *18*

Prep Time: *10* Minutes

Cook Time: *10* Minutes

Total Time: *20* Minutes

INGREDIENTS

- 1 ¾ cups flour
- 1 ¾ ground ginger
- ¼ tsp ground cinnamon
- 1/8 tsp nutmeg
- 1/8 tsp cloves
- 1 ½ tsp cornstarch
- ¼ cup milk
- ¼ cup molasses
- 3 tbs Swerve
- ¼ tsp salt
- 2 tbs butter
- 1 egg white
- 2 ¼ tsp vanilla
- 2 tsp stevia
- 1 tsp baking powder

DIRECTIONS

1. Preheat the oven to 325F.
2. Mix the cornstarch, nutmeg, flour, cloves, ginger, cinnamon, baking powder, and salt in a bowl.
3. In another bowl, whisk the butter, egg, vanilla, and stevia.
4. Stir in the molasses and milk.
5. Incorporate the flour mixture.
6. Divide into 18 portions and roll into balls.
7. Roll in the Swerve until coated.
8. Place on a lined baking sheet.
9. Sprinkle with Swerve and bake for 10 minutes.
10. Allow to cool, then serve.

Serves: *16*

Prep Time: *10*   Minutes

Cook Time: *60*   Minutes

Total Time: *70*   Minutes

INGREDIENTS

- **4 cups rice cereal**
- **2 tbs dark chocolate**
- **2/3 cup honey**
- **½ cup peanut butter**
- **Salt**
- **1 tsp vanilla**

DIRECTIONS

1. Combine all of the ingredients except for the dark chocolate in a bowl.
2. Spread the mixture on a lined baking pan.
3. Drizzle the melted chocolate on top.
4. Refrigerate for 1 hour.
5. Cut into bars and serve.

BREAKFAST COOKIES

Serves: **8-12**

Prep Time: **5** Minutes

Cook Time: **15** Minutes

Total Time: **20** Minutes

INGREDIENTS

- 1 cup rolled oats
- ¼ cup applesauce
- ½ tsp vanilla extract
- 3 tablespoons chocolate chips
- 2 tablespoons dried fruits
- 1 tsp cinnamon

DIRECTIONS

1. Preheat the oven to 325 F
2. In a bowl combine all ingredients together and mix well
3. Scoop cookies using an ice cream scoop
4. Place cookies onto a prepared baking sheet
5. Place in the oven for 12-15 minutes or until the cookies are done
6. When ready remove from the oven and serve

TANGERINE SMOOTHIE

Serves: **1**

Prep Time: **5**   Minutes

Cook Time: **5**   Minutes

Total Time: **10**   Minutes

INGREDIENTS

- 2 tangerines
- 1 cup pineapple
- 1 banana
- 1 cup ice

DIRECTIONS

1. In a blender place all ingredients and blend until smooth
2. Pour smoothie in a glass and serve

MOCKTAIL

Serves: *1*
Prep Time: *10*   Minutes

Cook Time: *0*   Minutes

Total Time: *10*   Minutes

INGREDIENTS

- Ice
- 6 ounces soda water
- 3 lime slices
- 11 mint leaves
- 1 tbs honey

DIRECTIONS

1. Add mint leaves and lime to a glass and muddle with a spoon.
2. Add honey, ice and soda.
3. Stir to combine.
4. Serve garnished with lime and mint.

PEANUT BUTTER SMOOTHIE

Serves: **1**

Prep Time: **5** Minutes

Cook Time: **5** Minutes

Total Time: **10** Minutes

INGREDIENTS

- 1 cup strawberries
- 1 banana
- 2 tablespoons peanut butter

DIRECTIONS

1. In a blender place all ingredients and blend until smooth
2. Pour smoothie in a glass and serve

CARROT SMOOTHIE

Serves: *1*

Prep Time: 5   Minutes

Cook Time: 5   Minutes

Total Time: *10*   Minutes

INGREDIENTS

- 1 carrot
- 1 mango
- 2 tablespoons coconut flakes

DIRECTIONS

1. In a blender place all ingredients and blend until smooth
2. Pour smoothie in a glass and serve

GINGER SMOOTHIE

Serves: *1*

Prep Time: *5*   Minutes

Cook Time: *5*   Minutes

Total Time: *10*   Minutes

INGREDIENTS

- 2 cups pineapple
- 2 tablespoons lime juice
- 1-pice ginger

DIRECTIONS

1. **In a blender place all ingredients and blend until smooth**
2. **Pour smoothie in a glass and serve**

KALE SMOOTHIE

Serves: *1*

Prep Time: 5   Minutes

Cook Time: 5   Minutes

Total Time: *10*   Minutes

INGREDIENTS

- 1 cup kale
- 1 cup cherries
- 1 cup blueberries

DIRECTIONS

1. In a blender place all ingredients and blend until smooth
2. Pour smoothie in a glass and serve

MANGO SMOOTHIE

Serves: *1*
Prep Time: 5   Minutes

Cook Time: 5   Minutes

Total Time: *10*   Minutes

INGREDIENTS

- 1 cup mango
- 1 cup cherries
- 1 cup Greek yogurt

DIRECTIONS

1. In a blender place all ingredients and blend until smooth
2. Pour smoothie in a glass and serve

SIMPLE MUFFINS

Serves: **8-12**

Prep Time: **10**   Minutes

Cook Time: **20**   Minutes

Total Time: **30**   Minutes

INGREDIENTS

- 2 eggs
- 1 tablespoon olive oil
- 1 cup milk
- 2 cups whole wheat flour
- 1 tsp baking soda
- ¼ tsp baking soda
- 1 cup pumpkin puree
- 1 tsp cinnamon
- ¼ cup molasses

DIRECTIONS

1. In a bowl combine all wet ingredients
2. In another bowl combine all dry ingredients

3. Combine wet and dry ingredients together
4. Pour mixture into 8-12 prepared muffin cups, fill 2/3 of the cups
5. Bake for 18-20 minutes at 375 F
6. When ready remove from the oven and serve

CORNBREAD MUFFINS

Serves: **4**

Prep Time: **10** Minutes

Cook Time: **20** Minutes

Total Time: **30** Minutes

INGREDIENTS

- **1 cup whole-wheat flour**
- **1 can of Whole Kernel Corn 15 oz.**
- **½ cup milk**
- **1 egg**
- **½ cup butter**
- **1 tablespoon honey**
- **1 tablespoon baking powder**
- **1 tsp salt**

DIRECTIONS

1. **Preheat oven to 375 F**
2. **Blend corn until smooth**
3. **In a bowl mix baking powder, salt and flour**
4. **In another bowl mix eggs, butter, corn, milk and honey**
5. **Pour over the flour mixture and mix well**
6. **Pour mixture into a cupcake pan and bake for 15-20 minutes**

Serves: *8-12*

Prep Time: *10*   Minutes

Cook Time: *25*   Minutes

Total Time: *35*   Minutes

INGREDIENTS

- 1 cup oats
- ¼ cup unsweetened applesauce
- 2 egg whites
- 1 cup oat milk
- 1 cup whole wheat flour
- ¼ cup brown sugar
- ¼ tsp baking soda
- ¼ tsp salt
- 1 tsp cinnamon
- ½ cup blueberries

DIRECTIONS

1. Preheat oven to 375 F
2. In a bowl combine all ingredients together and mix well
3. Fill 8-12 paper muffin cups with batter and fold in blueberries
4. Bake for 20-25 minutes, serve when ready

FIBER MUFFINS

Serves: **8-12**

Prep Time: **5** Minutes

Cook Time: **15** Minutes

Total Time: **20** Minutes

INGREDIENTS

- 1 cup wheat bran
- 1cup nonfat milk
- ¼ cup unsweetened applesauce
- 1 egg
- ¼ cup brown sugar
- ¼ cup all-purpose flour
- ¼ cup whole wheat flour
- 1 tsp baking powder
- 1 tsp baking soda
- ¼ tsp salt
- 1 cup blueberries

DIRECTIONS

1. Preheat oven to 400 F
2. In a bowl combine wheat bran and milk and set aside
3. In another bowl combine egg, brown sugar, apple sauce and stir in bran mixture, mix well

4. In another bowl combine baking soda, baking powder, wheat flour, all-purpose flour and mix well

5. Stir flour mixture into bran and egg mixture and mix well

6. Fold in blueberries and fill muffin cups with batter

7. Bake for 12-15 minutes

8. When ready remove and serve

STRAWBERRY MUFFINS

Serves: **8-12**
Prep Time: **10**   Minutes

Cook Time: **20**   Minutes

Total Time: **30**   Minutes

INGREDIENTS

- 2 eggs
- 1 tablespoon olive oil
- 1 cup milk
- 2 cups whole wheat flour
- 1 tsp baking soda
- ¼ tsp baking soda
- 1 tsp cinnamon
- 1 cup strawberries

DIRECTIONS

1. In a bowl combine all wet ingredients
2. In another bowl combine all dry ingredients
3. Combine wet and dry ingredients together
4. Fold in strawberries and mix well
5. Pour mixture into 8-12 prepared muffin cups, fill 2/3 of the cups
6. Bake for 18-20 minutes at 375 F, remove when ready

CHOCOLATE MUFFINS

Serves: *8-12*

Prep Time: *10*   Minutes

Cook Time: *20*   Minutes

Total Time: *30*   Minutes

INGREDIENTS

- 2 eggs
- 1 tablespoon olive oil
- 1 cup milk
- 2 cups whole wheat flour
- 1 tsp baking soda
- ¼ tsp baking soda
- 1 tsp cinnamon
- 1 cup chocolate chips

DIRECTIONS

1. In a bowl combine all wet ingredients
2. In another bowl combine all dry ingredients
3. Combine wet and dry ingredients together
4. Fold in chocolate chips and mix well
5. Pour mixture into 8-12 prepared muffin cups, fill 2/3 of the cups
6. Bake for 18-20 minutes at 375 F, remove when ready

SIMPLE MUFFINS

Serves: *8-12*
Prep Time: *10*   Minutes

Cook Time: *20*   Minutes

Total Time: *30*   Minutes

INGREDIENTS

- 2 eggs
- 1 tablespoon olive oil
- 1 cup milk
- 2 cups whole wheat flour
- 1 tsp baking soda
- ¼ tsp baking soda
- 1 tsp cinnamon

DIRECTIONS

1. In a bowl combine all wet ingredients
2. In another bowl combine all dry ingredients
3. Combine wet and dry ingredients together
4. Pour mixture into 8-12 prepared muffin cups, fill 2/3 of the cups
5. Bake for 18-20 minutes at 375 F
6. When ready remove from the oven and serve

THIRD COOKBOOK

PUMPKIN CUPCAKES

Serves: **4**
Prep Time: **10** Minutes

Cook Time: **30** Minutes

Total Time: **40** Minutes

INGREDIENTS

- 1 cup pumpkin puree
- 1 tsp cinnamon
- ½ tsp mixed spice
- 1 tsp ginger
- ¼ lb. butter
- 1 cups brown sugar
- 2 eggs
- 2 cups flour
- 3 tsp baking powder

DIRECTIONS

1. Boil the pumpkin and then puree in a food processor
2. Cream butter and sugar, add the eggs and beat well, stir in pureed pumpkin and dry ingredients
3. Combine all ingredients and spoon mixture into a muffin tin

4. Bake at 300 F for 20 minutes, remove and serve

BUCKWHEAT PANCAKES

Serves: **2**

Prep Time: **10** Minutes

Cook Time: **10** Minutes

Total Time: **20** Minutes

INGREDIENTS

- 1 cup buckwheat mix
- 1 egg
- 1 cup milk
- 1 tablespoon butter

DIRECTIONS

1. In a bow mix all ingredients, add olive oil and pour batter
2. Cook for 1-2 minutes per side
3. Remove and serve

CARROT CAKE

Serves: *4*

Prep Time: *10*   Minutes

Cook Time: *40*   Minutes

Total Time: *50*   Minutes

INGREDIENTS

- 1 cup whole meal self raising flour
- 1 cup brown sugar
- 1 cup self raising flour
- 1 tsp salt
- 1 tsp cinnamon
- 1 tsp ginger
- 1 cup olive oil
- 2 cups carrots
- 3 eggs
- ½ tsp allspice

DIRECTIONS

1. Preheat oven to 275 F and place all ingredients in a bowl except eggs
2. In another bowl mix eggs and add to the mixture
3. Pour into cake in
4. For carrot cake pour batter into cupcake molds

5. Bake for 40 minutes
6. Remove and serve

RUSSIAN FUDGE

Serves: **2**

Prep Time: **10**   Minutes

Cook Time: **30**   Minutes

Total Time: **40**   Minutes

INGREDIENTS

- ½ butter
- 1 can condensed milk
- ¾ cup milk
- 2 tablespoons golden syrup
- 3 cups sugar
- 1 tablespoon vanilla essence

DIRECTIONS

1. In a pot place all the ingredients except vanilla essence and bring to boil
2. Boil for 15-20 minutes and in another bowl drop some fudge mixture
3. Add vanilla essence and beat with a mixer for 5-6 minutes
4. Pour into greased tin and place in fridge
5. Cut into pieces and serve

Serves: *2*

Prep Time: *10*   Minutes

Cook Time: *20*   Minutes

Total Time: *30*   Minutes

INGREDIENTS

- 1-inch ginger
- 4 tablespoons brown sugar
- 1 tsp citric acid
- 1 L soda water
- fresh mint

DIRECTIONS

1. Grate ginger and mix with the rest of ingredients and let them sit for 10-12 minutes
2. Serve when ready

CINNAMON SCONES

Serves: **4**

Prep Time: **10** Minutes

Cook Time: **30** Minutes

Total Time: **40** Minutes

INGREDIENTS

- 2 cups self raising flour
- 2 tablespoons butter
- 2/3 cups milk

FILLING

- 1/3 cup butter
- ¾ cup brown sugar
- 1 tsp cinnamon

DIRECTIONS

1. Preheat oven to 350 F
2. In a blender add butter, flour and blend until smooth
3. Add milk and blend or another 1-2 minutes
4. Remove mixture onto floured surface
5. In the blender put all ingredients for the filling and blend until smooth
6. Spread the filling into the dough

MAC AND CHEESELESS

Serves: *4*

Prep Time: *10*   Minutes

Cook Time: *30*   Minutes

Total Time: *40*   Minutes

INGREDIENTS

- 1 leek
- 1 clove garlic
- sat
- citric acid
- 1 tsp turmeric
- 1 tsp cumin
- 1 tsp coriander powder
- ½ cup roasted sunflower seeds
- 1 tablespoon rice flour
- 1 tsp arrowroot
- 1 cup broccoli
- 2 tablespoons butter
- 1 cup milk
- macaroni pasta

DIRECTIONS

1. Cook pasta, add leek and sauté with butter, citric acid and pepper
2. Add butter, cumin, coriander powder, turmeric, sunflower seeds
3. Add arrowroot and rice flour and cook for 2-3 minutes
4. Add broccoli, pasta and stir
5. Cook for 20 minutes at 350 F, remove and serve

SPRING ROLLS

Serves: *4*
Prep Time: *10*   Minutes

Cook Time: *20*   Minutes

Total Time: *30*   Minutes

INGREDIENTS

- rice noodles
- onion
- cucumber
- carrot
- Coriander
- zucchini
- carrot
- Thai mint
- Chives
- Roasted sunflower seeds
- ginger
- rice paper
- tofu

DIRECTIONS

1. In a bowl place the noodles and boil, cover with a lid

2. When they are cool set aside, soak a couple of rice papers in warm water and place the rice paper on a towel

3. Place the noodles and the rest of rest of ingredients on a rice paper and fold

4. Serve when ready

GINGER CRUNCH

Serves: *4*
Prep Time: *10*   Minutes

Cook Time: *30*   Minutes

Total Time: *40*   Minutes

INGREDIENTS

- ¼ lb. butter
- ½ cup sugar
- 1 cup plain flour
- ½ whole meal flour
- 1 tsp baking powder
- 1 tsp ginger

DIRECTIONS

1. In a food processor add butter and soon and blend until smooth
2. Add the rest of ingredients and blend
3. Remove from blender and bake for 20 minutes at 350 F
4. Cut into cookie shape and serve

CORNMEAL WAFFELS

Serves: *2*

Prep Time: *10*   Minutes

Cook Time: *10*   Minutes

Total Time: *20*   Minutes

INGREDIENTS

- 1 cup corn flour
- 1 egg
- 1 cup milk
- 1 tablespoon butter
- 2 tablespoons honey
- ½ cup rice flour
- 1 tsp baking powder
- ½ tsp salt

DIRECTIONS

1. Let sit for 8-10 minutes
2. Place in the waffle iron and cook
3. Remove and serve

CHEESE CAKE

Serves: **4**

Prep Time: **10** Minutes

Cook Time: **30** Minutes

Total Time: **40** Minutes

INGREDIENTS

- ½ lb. gingernut biscuits
- ½ lb. blueberries
- 1 tsp vanilla extract
- 1 tsp acid
- ¼ lb. butter
- ¼ lb. caster sugar
- 2 tablespoons arrowroot
- ¼ lb. full-fat Philadelphia
- 2 eggs

DIRECTIONS

1. Preheat oven to 350 F
2. In a bowl mix butter and biscuits and press into the base of the tin
3. Bake for 10-12 minutes
4. In a saucepan cook blueberry with sugar and milk for 10-12 minutes

5. Take off heat add citric acid and vanilla
6. Bake for 40 minutes remove and let it chill

Serves: **2**

Prep Time: **10**   Minutes

Cook Time: **10**   Minutes

Total Time: **20**   Minutes

INGREDIENTS

- 2 eggs
- 1 tablespoon sugar
- 1 tablespoon baking powder
- 1 cup flour
- 1/8 cup milk
- ½ tsp vanilla essence

DIRECTIONS

1. In a food processor add all the ingredients and blend until smooth
2. Heat the waffle iron pour in the batter
3. Cook until golden
4. Serve with maple syrup

CARAMEL POPCORN

Serves: **4**

Prep Time: **10**   Minutes

Cook Time: **20**   Minutes

Total Time: **30**   Minutes

INGREDIENTS

- 1 tablespoon olive oil
- 4 tablespoons popcorn kernels

CARAMEL SAUCE

- 1 tablespoon butter
- 1 tablespoon brown sugar
- 1 tablespoon golden syrup

DIRECTIONS

1. In a saucepan pour olive oil and popcorn kernels over medium heat and cover
2. Shake the saucepan to distribute evenly
3. In another saucepan melt the caramel sauce ingredients
4. Remove from heat and pour over your popcorn

Serves: *4*

Prep Time: *10*   Minutes

Cook Time: *10*   Minutes

Total Time: *20*   Minutes

INGREDIENTS

- ½ tsp salt
- 1 cup plain flour
- 1 tsp olive oil
- 1 onion
- ½ cup hot water
- 1 tablespoon cold water

DIRECTIONS

1. In a bowl mix all ingredients
2. Pour mixture into a pan and cook for 1-2 minutes per side
3. Remove and serve

TOASTED MUESLI

Serves: **4**

Prep Time: **10**   Minutes

Cook Time: **60**   Minutes

Total Time: **70**   Minutes

INGREDIENTS

- 2 cups oats
- 1 cup oat mix
- ½ cup sunflower seeds
- ½ cup sunflower oil

DIRECTIONS

1. In a bowl mix all ingredients
2. Bake for 60 minutes at 275 F
3. Garnish with blueberries and serve

GINGERBREAD BISCUITS

Serves: **4**

Prep Time: **10**   Minutes

Cook Time: **30**   Minutes

Total Time: **40**   Minutes

INGREDIENTS

- 2 oz. butter
- 1 cup self raising flour
- ½ tsp salt
- 3 tablespoons ginger
- ½ cup milk
- 1 egg beaten
- 1 tablespoon vanilla extract
- ½ cup golden syrup
- ½ cup maple syrup
- ½ cup honey

DIRECTIONS

1. Preheat oven to 300 F
2. In a pan melt honey, butter, syrup and set aside
3. White syrup mixture is cooling, grate the ginger and add to the syrup mixture
4. Add flour, salt, milk, egg and vanilla extract

5. Form small cookies and bake for 15-18 minutes at 300 F

6. Remove and serve

VANILLA CHIA PUDDING

Serves: *4*
Prep Time: *10* Minutes

Cook Time: *10* Minutes

Total Time: *20* Minutes

INGREDIENTS

- 2 cups hemp milk
- 2 packets stevia
- ½ tsp cinnamon
- ½ cup chia seeds
- 1 tablespoon vanilla extract

DIRECTIONS

1. In a bowl whisk all ingredients together
2. Let it chill overnight and serve

APPLE PANCAKES

Serves: **4**

Prep Time: **10**   Minutes

Cook Time: **20**   Minutes

Total Time: **30**   Minutes

INGREDIENTS

- 1 cup whole wheat flour
- ¼ tsp baking soda
- ¼ tsp baking powder
- 1 cup apples
- 2 eggs
- 1 cup milk

DIRECTIONS

1. In a bowl combine all ingredients together and mix well
2. In a skillet heat olive oil
3. Pour ¼ of the batter and cook each pancake for 1-2 minutes per side
4. When ready remove from heat and serve

APRICOTS PANCAKES

Serves: *4*

Prep Time: *10*   Minutes

Cook Time: *30*   Minutes

Total Time: *40*   Minutes

INGREDIENTS

- 1 cup whole wheat flour
- ¼ tsp baking soda
- ¼ tsp baking powder
- 1 cup apricots
- 2 eggs
- 1 cup milk

DIRECTIONS

1. In a bowl combine all ingredients together and mix well
2. In a skillet heat olive oil
3. Pour ¼ of the batter and cook each pancake for 1-2 minutes per side
4. When ready remove from heat and serve

ACEROLA PANCAKES

Serves: **4**

Prep Time: **10**   Minutes

Cook Time: **20**   Minutes

Total Time: **30**   Minutes

INGREDIENTS

- 1 cup whole wheat flour
- ¼ tsp baking soda
- ¼ tsp baking powder
- 1 cup acerola
- 2 eggs
- 1 cup milk

DIRECTIONS

1. In a bowl combine all ingredients together and mix well
2. In a skillet heat olive oil
3. Pour ¼ of the batter and cook each pancake for 1-2 minutes per side
4. When ready remove from heat and serve

JAVA-PLUM MUFFINS

Serves: **8-12**

Prep Time: **10**   Minutes

Cook Time: **20**   Minutes

Total Time: **30**   Minutes

INGREDIENTS

- 2 eggs
- 1 tablespoon olive oil
- 1 cup milk
- 2 cups whole wheat flour
- 1 tsp baking soda
- ¼ tsp baking soda
- 1 tsp cinnamon
- 1 cup java-plum

DIRECTIONS

1. In a bowl combine all wet ingredients
2. In another bowl combine all dry ingredients
3. Combine wet and dry ingredients together
4. Pour mixture into 8-12 prepared muffin cups, fill 2/3 of the cups
5. Bake for 18-20 minutes at 375 F
6. When ready remove from the oven and serve

Serves: *8-12*

Prep Time: *10*   Minutes

Cook Time: *20*   Minutes

Total Time: *30*   Minutes

INGREDIENTS

- 2 eggs
- 1 tablespoon olive oil
- 1 cup milk
- 2 cups whole wheat flour
- 1 tsp baking soda
- ¼ tsp baking soda
- 1 tsp cinnamon
- 1 cup kiwi

DIRECTIONS

1. In a bowl combine all wet ingredients
2. In another bowl combine all dry ingredients
3. Combine wet and dry ingredients together
4. Pour mixture into 8-12 prepared muffin cups, fill 2/3 of the cups
5. Bake for 18-20 minutes at 375 F
6. When ready remove from the oven and serve

CHOCOLATE MUFFINS

Serves: **8-12**

Prep Time: **10** Minutes

Cook Time: **20** Minutes

Total Time: **30** Minutes

INGREDIENTS

- 2 eggs
- 1 tablespoon olive oil
- 1 cup milk
- 2 cups whole wheat flour
- 1 tsp baking soda
- ¼ tsp baking soda
- 1 tsp cinnamon
- 1 cup chocolate chips

DIRECTIONS

1. In a bowl combine all wet ingredients
2. In another bowl combine all dry ingredients
3. Combine wet and dry ingredients together
4. Pour mixture into 8-12 prepared muffin cups, fill 2/3 of the cups
5. Bake for 18-20 minutes at 375 F
6. When ready remove from the oven and serve

MANGO MUFFINS

Serves: **8-12**

Prep Time: **10**   Minutes

Cook Time: **20**   Minutes

Total Time: **30**   Minutes

INGREDIENTS

- 2 eggs
- 1 tablespoon olive oil
- 1 cup milk
- 2 cups whole wheat flour
- 1 tsp baking soda
- ¼ tsp baking soda
- 1 tsp cinnamon
- 1 cup mango

DIRECTIONS

1. In a bowl combine all wet ingredients
2. In another bowl combine all dry ingredients
3. Combine wet and dry ingredients together
4. Pour mixture into 8-12 prepared muffin cups, fill 2/3 of the cups
5. Bake for 18-20 minutes at 375 F
6. When ready remove from the oven and serve

BOK CHOY OMELETTE

Serves: *1*

Prep Time: *5*   Minutes

Cook Time: *10*   Minutes

Total Time: *15*   Minutes

INGREDIENTS

- 2 eggs
- ¼ tsp salt
- ¼ tsp black pepper
- 1 tablespoon olive oil
- ¼ cup cheese
- ¼ tsp basil
- 1 cup bok choy

DIRECTIONS

1. In a bowl combine all ingredients together and mix well
2. In a skillet heat olive oil and pour the egg mixture
3. Cook for 1-2 minutes per side
4. When ready remove omelette from the skillet and serve

BRUSSEL SPROUTS OMELETTE

Serves: *1*

Prep Time: *5*   Minutes

Cook Time: *10*   Minutes

Total Time: *15*   Minutes

INGREDIENTS

- 2 eggs
- ¼ tsp salt
- ¼ tsp black pepper
- 1 tablespoon olive oil
- ¼ cup cheese
- ¼ tsp basil
- 1 cup Brussel sprouts

DIRECTIONS

1. In a bowl combine all ingredients together and mix well
2. In a skillet heat olive oil and pour the egg mixture
3. Cook for 1-2 minutes per side
4. When ready remove omelette from the skillet and serve

CARROT OMELETTE

Serves: *1*
Prep Time: *5*   Minutes
Cook Time: *10* Minutes
Total Time: *15* Minutes

INGREDIENTS

- 2 eggs
- ¼ tsp salt
- ¼ tsp black pepper
- 1 tablespoon olive oil
- ¼ cup cheese
- ¼ tsp basil
- 1 cup carrot

DIRECTIONS

1. In a bowl combine all ingredients together and mix well
2. In a skillet heat olive oil and pour the egg mixture
3. Cook for 1-2 minutes per side
4. When ready remove omelette from the skillet and serve

CORN OMELETTE

Serves: **1**

Prep Time: **5**   Minutes

Cook Time: **10**   Minutes

Total Time: **15**   Minutes

INGREDIENTS

- 2 eggs
- ¼ tsp salt
- ¼ tsp black pepper
- 1 tablespoon olive oil
- ¼ cup cheese
- ¼ tsp basil
- 1 cup corn

DIRECTIONS

1. In a bowl combine all ingredients together and mix well
2. In a skillet heat olive oil and pour the egg mixture
3. Cook for 1-2 minutes per side
4. When ready remove omelette from the skillet and serve

EGGPLANT OMELETTE

Serves: *1*

Prep Time: *5*   Minutes

Cook Time: *10* Minutes

Total Time: *15* Minutes

INGREDIENTS

- 2 eggs
- ¼ tsp salt
- ¼ tsp black pepper
- 1 tablespoon olive oil
- ¼ cup cheese
- ¼ tsp basil
- 1 cup eggplant

DIRECTIONS

1. In a bowl combine all ingredients together and mix well
2. In a skillet heat olive oil and pour the egg mixture
3. Cook for 1-2 minutes per side
4. When ready remove omelette from the skillet and serve

TART RECIPES

APPLE TART

Serves: **6-8**

Prep Time: **25**   Minutes

Cook Time: **25**   Minutes

Total Time: **50**   Minutes

INGREDIENTS

- pastry sheets

FILLING

- 1 tsp lemon juice
- 3 oz. brown sugar
- 1 lb. apples
- 150 ml double cream
- 2 eggs

DIRECTIONS

1. Preheat oven to 400 F, unfold pastry sheets and place them on a baking sheet
2. Toss together all ingredients together and mix well
3. Spread mixture in a single layer on the pastry sheets
4. Before baking decorate with your desired fruits
5. Bake at 400 F for 22-25 minutes or until golden brown

6. When ready remove from the oven and serve

CHOCHOLATE TART

Serves: *6-8*
Prep Time: *25*   Minutes

Cook Time: *25*   Minutes

Total Time: *50*   Minutes

INGREDIENTS

- pastry sheets
- 1 tsp vanilla extract
- ½ lb. caramel
- ½ lb. black chocolate
- 4-5 tablespoons butter
- 3 eggs
- ¼ lb. brown sugar

DIRECTIONS

1. Preheat oven to 400 F, unfold pastry sheets and place them on a baking sheet
2. Toss together all ingredients together and mix well
3. Spread mixture in a single layer on the pastry sheets
4. Before baking decorate with your desired fruits
5. Bake at 400 F for 22-25 minutes or until golden brown
6. When ready remove from the oven and serve

PEACH PECAN PIE

Serves: **8-12**

Prep Time: **15**   Minutes

Cook Time: **35**   Minutes

Total Time: **50**   Minutes

INGREDIENTS

- 4-5 cups peaches
- 1 tablespoon preserves
- 1 cup sugar
- 4 small egg yolks
- ¼ cup flour
- 1 tsp vanilla extract

DIRECTIONS

1. Line a pie plate or pie form with pastry and cover the edges of the plate depending on your preference
2. In a bowl combine all pie ingredients together and mix well
3. Pour the mixture over the pastry
4. Bake at 400-425 F for 25-30 minutes or until golden brown
5. When ready remove from the oven and let it rest for 15 minutes

OREO PIE

Serves: *8-12*

Prep Time: *15*   Minutes

Cook Time: *35*   Minutes

Total Time: *50*   Minutes

INGREDIENTS

- pastry sheets
- 6-8 oz. chocolate crumb piecrust
- 1 cup half-and-half
- 1 package instant pudding mix
- 10-12 Oreo cookies
- 10 oz. whipped topping

DIRECTIONS

1. Line a pie plate or pie form with pastry and cover the edges of the plate depending on your preference
2. In a bowl combine all pie ingredients together and mix well
3. Pour the mixture over the pastry
4. Bake at 400-425 F for 25-30 minutes or until golden brown
5. When ready remove from the oven and let it rest for 15 minutes

GRAPEFRUIT PIE

Serves: *8-12*
Prep Time: *15*   Minutes

Cook Time: *35*   Minutes

Total Time: *50*   Minutes

INGREDIENTS

- pastry sheets
- 2 cups grapefruit
- 1 cup brown sugar
- ¼ cup flour
- 5-6 egg yolks
- 5 oz. butter

DIRECTIONS

1. Line a pie plate or pic form with pastry and cover the edges of the plate depending on your preference
2. In a bowl combine all pie ingredients together and mix well
3. Pour the mixture over the pastry
4. Bake at 400-425 F for 25-30 minutes or until golden brown
5. When ready remove from the oven and let it rest for 15 minutes

BUTTERFINGER PIE

Serves: **8-12**

Prep Time: **15** Minutes

Cook Time: **35** Minutes

Total Time: **50** Minutes

INGREDIENTS

- pastry sheets
- 1 package cream cheese
- 1 tsp vanilla extract
- ¼ cup peanut butter
- 1 cup powdered sugar (to decorate)
- 2 cups Butterfinger candy bars
- 8 oz whipped topping

DIRECTIONS

1. Line a pie plate or pie form with pastry and cover the edges of the plate depending on your preference
2. In a bowl combine all pie ingredients together and mix well
3. Pour the mixture over the pastry
4. Bake at 400-425 F for 25-30 minutes or until golden brown
5. When ready remove from the oven and let it rest for 15 minutes

CREAMSICLE SMOOTHIE

Serves: **1**
Prep Time: **5**   Minutes

Cook Time: **5**   Minutes

Total Time: **10** Minutes

INGREDIENTS

- 2 cups mango
- 1 carrot
- 1 tablespoon apple cider vinegar
- 1 tsp lemon juice
- 1 cup coconut milk
- 1 tsp honey

DIRECTIONS

1. In a blender place all ingredients and blend until smooth
2. Pour smoothie in a glass and serve

BUTTERMILK SMOOTHIE

Serves: *1*

Prep Time: 5   Minutes

Cook Time: 5   Minutes

Total Time: *10*   Minutes

INGREDIENTS

- 1 cup strawberries
- 1 cup buttermilk
- 1 cup ice
- 1 tsp honey
- 1 tsp agave syrup

DIRECTIONS

1. In a blender place all ingredients and blend until smooth
2. Pour smoothie in a glass and serve

PARSLEY & PINEAPPLE SMOOTHIE

Serves: **1**

Prep Time: **5** Minutes

Cook Time: **5** Minutes

Total Time: **10** Minutes

INGREDIENTS

- 1 banana
- 1 cup pineapple
- ¼ cup parsley
- 1 tsp chia seeds
- 1 cup ice

DIRECTIONS

1. In a blender place all ingredients and blend until smooth
2. Pour smoothie in a glass and serve

POMEGRANATE SMOOTHIE

Serves: *1*

Prep Time: 5   Minutes

Cook Time: 5   Minutes

Total Time: *10*   Minutes

INGREDIENTS

- 1 cup pomegranate juice
- ¼ cup vanilla yogurt
- 3 cooked beets
- ¼ cup grapefruit juice
- 1 tablespoon honey
- 1 cup ice

DIRECTIONS

1. In a blender place all ingredients and blend until smooth
2. Pour smoothie in a glass and serve

CASHEW SMOOTHIE

Serves: *1*

Prep Time: 5   Minutes

Cook Time: 5   Minutes

Total Time: *10*   Minutes

INGREDIENTS

- 1 cup cashew milk
- 1 cup vanilla yogurt
- 1 banana
- 1 cup pumpkin puree
- 1 cup ice

DIRECTIONS

1. In a blender place all ingredients and blend until smooth
2. Pour smoothie in a glass and serve

ICE-CREAM RECIPES

PISTACHIOS ICE-CREAM

Serves: **6-8**

Prep Time: **15**   Minutes

Cook Time: **15**   Minutes

Total Time: **30**   Minutes

INGREDIENTS

- 4 egg yolks
- 1 cup heavy cream
- 1 cup milk
- 1 cup sugar
- 1 vanilla bean
- 1 tsp almond extract
- 1 cup cherries
- ½ cup pistachios

DIRECTIONS

1. In a saucepan whisk together all ingredients
2. Mix until bubbly
3. Strain into a bowl and cool
4. Whisk in favorite fruits and mix well
5. Cover and refrigerate for 2-3 hours

6. Pour mixture in the ice-cream maker and follow manufacturer instructions

7. Serve when ready

VANILLA ICE-CREAM

Serves: **6-8**

Prep Time: **15**   Minutes

Cook Time: **15**   Minutes

Total Time: **30**   Minutes

INGREDIENTS

- 1 cup milk
- 1 tablespoon cornstarch
- 1 oz. cream cheese
- 1 cup heavy cream
- 1 cup brown sugar
- 1 tablespoon corn syrup
- 1 vanilla bean

DIRECTIONS

1. In a saucepan whisk together all ingredients
2. Mix until bubbly
3. Strain into a bowl and cool
4. Whisk in favorite fruits and mix well
5. Cover and refrigerate for 2-3 hours
6. Pour mixture in the ice-cream maker and follow manufacturer instructions
7. Serve when ready

FOURTH COOKBOOK

MINESTRONE SOUP

Serves: *6*

Prep Time: *10*   Minutes

Cook Time: *50*   Minutes

Total Time: *60*   Minutes

INGREDIENTS

-   2 onions
-   1 cup peas
-   1 can tomatoes
-   2 cups tomato sauce
-   3 carrots
-   1 cup green beans
-   2 tbs basil
-   6 cups water
-   2 cloves garlic
-   Salt
-   2 tbs cheese
-   1.5 cups kidney
-   2 cups celery
-   1 bell pepper

DIRECTIONS

1. Put the onions, celery and carrots into a pot of water.

2. Add the green beans, peas, tomatoes and bell pepper when the water starts to boil, then allow to boil for 30 minutes.

3. Add the tomato sauce and basil then season with salt.

4. Allow to simmer for 10 minutes, then add the garlic and simmer for 5 more minutes.

5. Serve topped with cheese.

TUNA SALAD

Serves: *4*

Prep Time: *10*   Minutes

Cook Time: *5*   Minutes

Total Time: *15*   Minutes

INGREDIENTS
- ½ tsp lemon zest
- Salt
- Pepper
- 4 eggs
- 1/3 red onion
- ¾ lb green beans
- 1 can tuna
- 1 tsp oregano
- 6 tbs olive oil
- 3 tbs lemon juice
- 1 can beans
- 1 can black olives

DIRECTIONS

1. Place the green beans, 1/3 cup water and salt to taste in a skillet.
2. Bring to a boil, covered.
3. Cook for 5 minutes.

4. Dump them onto a lined cookie sheet.

5. Mix the white beans, onion, olives and tuna.

6. Combine the oregano, lemon juice and zest, and oil in a separate bowl.

7. Pour the mixture over the tuna mixture.

8. Season and serve immediately with the boiled eggs.

CHICKEN SKILLET

Serves: **4**

Prep Time: **10** Minutes

Cook Time: **30** Minutes

Total Time: **40** Minutes

INGREDIENTS

- **1 tsp oil**
- **½ cup carrots**
- **1 zucchini**
- **1 bell pepper**
- **½ lb chicken**
- **1 onion**

DIRECTIONS

1. Cut the chicken into strips, then cook in the oil until it gets brown.
2. Remove from the skillet and add the vegetables.
3. Cook until soft for 10 minutes, then add the chicken.
4. Season and serve immediately.

SPINACH QUESADILLAS

Serves: *4*

Prep Time: *10*   Minutes

Cook Time: *15*   Minutes

Total Time: *25*   Minutes

INGREDIENTS

- 4 cups spinach
- 4 green onions
- 1 tomato
- ½ lemon juice
- 1 tsp cumin
- 1 tsp garlic powder
- Salt
- 1 cup cheese
- 4 tortillas

DIRECTIONS

1. Cook all of the ingredients except for the cheese and tortillas in a skillet.
2. Cook until the spinach is wilted.
3. Remove to a bowl and add the cheese.
4. Place the mixture on half of the tortilla, fold the other half and cook for 2 minutes on each side on a griddle

BEAN SALAD

Serves: *4*
Prep Time: *10*   Minutes

Cook Time: *0*   Minutes

Total Time: *10*   Minutes

INGREDIENTS

- 1 can garbanzo beans
- 1 can red beans
- 1 tomato
- ½ red onion
- ½ lemon juice
- 1 tbs olive oil

DIRECTIONS

1. Mix all of the ingredients together in a bowl.
2. Season with salt and serve immediately.

GARLIC SALMON

Serves: *4*
Prep Time: *10*   Minutes

Cook Time: *20*   Minutes

Total Time: *30*   Minutes

INGREDIENTS

- **2 lb salmon**
- **2 tbs water**
- **Salt**
- **2 tbs parsley**
- **4 cloves garlic**

DIRECTIONS

1. Preheat the oven to 400F.
2. Mix the garlic, parsley, salt and water in a bowl.
3. Brush the mixture over the salmon.
4. Place the fish on a baking tray and cover with aluminum foil.
5. Cook for 20 minutes.
6. Serve with vegetables.

TUNA WRAP

Serves: **4**

Prep Time: **10**   Minutes

Cook Time: **0**   Minutes

Total Time: **10**   Minutes

INGREDIENTS

- **6 ounces tuna**
- **2 tsp yogurt**
- **½ celery stalk**
- **Handful baby spinach**
- **½ onion**
- **2 tsp lemon juice**
- **4 tortillas**

DIRECTIONS

1. Mix all of the ingredients except for the tortillas in a bowl.
2. Spread the mixture over the tortillas, then wrap them up.
3. Serve immediately.

ROASTED CHICKEN WRAP

Serves: **4**

Prep Time: **10**   Minutes

Cook Time: **10**   Minutes

Total Time: **20**   Minutes

INGREDIENTS

- **1 cup chicken breast**
- **2 tsp yogurt**
- **1/3 cup celery**
- **8 tomato slices**
- **½ onion**
- **1 tbs mustard**
- **2 tbs ketchup**
- **4 tortillas**

DIRECTIONS

1. **Cut the chicken as you desire and grill until done on each side.**
2. **Mix all of the ingredients except for the tortillas in a bowl.**
3. **Spread the mixture over the tortillas and add the chicken.**
4. **Serve immediately.**

Serves: **4**

Prep Time: **10**   Minutes

Cook Time: **0**   Minutes

Total Time: **10**   Minutes

INGREDIENTS

- **1 cup cooked lentils**
- **1 cup baby spinach**
- **1 poached egg**
- **¼ avocado**
- **½ tomato**
- **1-2 slices whole wheat bread**

DIRECTIONS

1. **Mix all of the ingredients together except for the bread.**
2. **Toast the bread.**
3. **Serve immediately together.**

STUFFED EGGPLANT

Serves: **4**

Prep Time: **10**   Minutes

Cook Time: **50**   Minutes

Total Time: **60**   Minutes

INGREDIENTS
- 1 eggplant
- 2 onions
- 1 red pepper
- ½ cup tomato juice
- ¼ cup cheese

DIRECTIONS

1. Preheat the oven to 350F.
2. Cut the eggplant in half and cook for 30 minutes.
3. Cook the diced onion in 2 tbs of water until brown.
4. Add the pepper and add it to the onion, cooking for another 5 minutes.
5. Add the tomato juice and allow to cook for another 5 minutes.
6. Scoop out the eggplant.
7. Mix the eggplant with the onion mixture, then add it back into the eggplant shell.
8. Grate the cheese on top and bake for another 10 minutes.
9. Serve hot.

BROCCOLI & AURGULA SOUP

Serves: 2

Prep Time: 5   Minutes

Cook Time: 20   Minutes

Total Time: 25   Minutes

INGREDIENTS

- 1 tbs olive oil
- ¼ tsp thyme
- 1 cup arugula
- ½ lemon juice
- 1 head broccoli
- 1 clove garlic
- 2 cups water
- ¼ tsp salt
- ¼ tsp black pepper
- ½ yellow onion

DIRECTIONS

1. Heat the oil in a saucepan.
2. Cook the onion until soft, then add the garlic and cook for another minute.
3. Add the broccoli and cook for 5 minutes.
4. Add the water, thyme, salt, and pepper.

5. Bring to boil, then lower the heat and cook for 10 minutes.
6. Transfer to a blender, blend, then add the arugula and blend until smooth.
7. Add the lemon juice and serve immediately.

STUFFED PEPPERS

Serves: **4**

Prep Time: **20**   Minutes

Cook Time: **25**   Minutes

Total Time: **45**   Minutes

INGREDIENTS

- ½ onion
- 1 cup mushrooms
- ½ yellow bell pepper
- 1 cup spinach
- 1 can tomatoes
- 1 tbs tomato paste
- 4 red bell peppers
- 1 lb ground turkey
- 2 tbs olive oil
- 1 zucchini
- ½ green bell pepper
- 1 tsp Italian seasoning
- ½ tsp garlic powder
- Salt
- Pepper

DIRECTIONS

1. Bring a pot of water to a boil.
2. Cut the tops off the peppers, and remove the seeds.
3. Cook in water for 5 minutes.
4. Preheat the oven to 350F.
5. Cook the turkey until brown.
6. Heat the oil and cook the onion, mushrooms, zucchini, green and yellow pepper, and spinach until soft.
7. Add the turkey and the rest of the ingredients.
8. Stuff the peppers with the mixture.
9. Bake for 15 minutes.
10. Serve hot.

POTATO SALAD

Serves: **6**

Prep Time: **5**   Minutes

Cook Time: **10**   Minutes

Total Time: **15**   Minutes

INGREDIENTS

- 1 red onion
- 2 tsp cumin seeds
- 1 cloves garlic
- ½ cup olive oil
- 4 potatoes
- ½ cup lemon juice
- 2 tbs fresh parsley
- 1 ½ tsp salt
- 2 tsp turmeric powder

DIRECTIONS

1. Steam the potatoes for 10 minutes, until tender.
2. Mix the lemon juice, turmeric, cumin seeds, and salt.
3. Place the potatoes in a bowl and pour the mixture over.
4. Add the onion and garlic and stir to coat.
5. Refrigerate until the potatoes are cold.

6. Add olive oil and herbs and stir.

PORK TACOS

Serves: *4*
Prep Time: *20*   Minutes

Cook Time: *10*   Minutes

Total Time: *30*   Minutes

INGREDIENTS

- 1 cucumber
- 1 cup red cabbage
- 1 ½ lbs ground pork
- 6 radishes
- 4 tsp sugar
- 2 tbs olive oil
- ¼ cup white wine vinegar
- 2 tbs soy sauce
- 2 tsp garlic powder
- 2 tbs sesame oil
- 4 scallions
- 2 tsp Sriracha
- 12 tortillas
- 2 tsp cilantro
- ½ cup sour cream
- Salt
- Pepper

DIRECTIONS

1. Place the cucumbers, radishes, vinegar, 2 tsp sugar, salt, and pepper in a bowl.

2. Cook the scallions and cabbage in the oil until soft.

3. Add the pork, garlic powder, and 2 tsp sugar and cook for another 5 minutes.

4. Add the sesame oil, Sriracha, soy sauce and combine.

5. Season with salt and pepper.

6. Heat the tortillas in the microwave for a few seconds.

7. Spread sour cream on the tortilla, add the mixture, sprinkle cilantro over and add the cucumber and radishes.

8. Serve immediately.

GREEK LAMB MEATBALLS

Serves: **4**

Prep Time: **10**   Minutes

Cook Time: **25**   Minutes

Total Time: **40**   Minutes

INGREDIENTS

- 1 lb. ground lamb
- 1 egg
- 1 cloves garlic
- 1 handful parsley
- 1 tablespoon dried oregano
- 1 tsp dried rosemary
- ½ cup fetta cheese
- ¼ tsp salt

DIRECTIONS

1. Preheat the oven to 325 F
2. In a bowl mix all ingredients
3. Form into meat balls
4. Bake for 20-25 minutes, remove and serve

BAKED CHILLI CHICKEN

Serves: *4*

Prep Time: *10*   Minutes

Cook Time: *30*   Minutes

Total Time: *40*   Minutes

INGREDIENTS

- 2 lb. chicken drumsticks
- 3 tablespoons olive oil
- 2 cloves garlic
- 2 tablespoons lime juice
- 3 tsp lime zest
- 1 tsp chilli flakes
- salt

DIRECTIONS

1. In a bowl place all ingredients except chicken drumsticks
2. Refrigerate and then add the drumsticks for 1-2 hours
3. Preheat oven to 350 F
4. Arrange the chicken drumsticks on a greased oven tray and bake for 40-45 minutes
5. Remove and serve

BROCCOLI STIR FRY

Serves: **2**

Prep Time: **10** Minutes

Cook Time: **15** Minutes

Total Time: **25** Minutes

INGREDIENTS

- 1 head broccoli
- 1 handful cashews
- 1 tablespoons macadamia nut oil
- 2 tablespoons coconut aminos
- 1 tablespoon fish sauce
- 2 cloves garlic
- ¼ red pepper
- 1 tablespoon lime juice
- 6 oz. shrimp
- 1 tablespoon sesame seeds
- salt

DIRECTIONS

1. In a frying pan heat oil over medium heat
2. Add garlic, sesame seeds, red pepper and cashews
3. Add shrimp and fry for 3-4 minutes

4. Remove and serve

SPINACH FRITATTA

Serves: **2**
Prep Time: **10**   Minutes

Cook Time: **20**   Minutes

Total Time: **30**   Minutes

INGREDIENTS

- ½ lb. spinach
- 1 tablespoon olive oil
- ½ red onion
- 2 eggs
- ¼ tsp salt
- 2 oz. cheddar cheese
- 1 garlic clove
- ¼ tsp dill

DIRECTIONS

1. In a bowl whisk eggs with salt and cheese
2. In a frying pan heat olive oil and pour egg mixture
3. Add remaining ingredients and mix well
4. Serve when ready

TURNIP FRITATTA

Serves: *2*
Prep Time: *10*   Minutes

Cook Time: *20*   Minutes

Total Time: *30*   Minutes

INGREDIENTS

- ½ lb. spinach
- ¼ cup turnip
- ½ red onion
- 2 eggs
- ¼ tsp salt
- 2 oz. cheddar cheese
- 1 garlic clove
- ¼ tsp dill

DIRECTIONS

1. In a bowl whisk eggs with salt and cheese
2. In a frying pan heat olive oil and pour egg mixture
3. Add remaining ingredients and mix well
4. Serve when ready

SQUASH FRITATTA

Serves: **2**

Prep Time: **10**   Minutes

Cook Time: **20**   Minutes

Total Time: **30**   Minutes

INGREDIENTS

- 1 cup squash
- 1 tablespoon olive oil
- ½ red onion
- 2 eggs
- ¼ tsp salt
- 2 oz. cheddar cheese
- 1 garlic clove
- ¼ tsp dill

DIRECTIONS

1. In a bowl whisk eggs with salt and cheese
2. In a frying pan heat olive oil and pour egg mixture
3. Add remaining ingredients and mix well
4. Serve when ready

HAM FRITATTA

Serves: **2**

Prep Time: **10** Minutes

Cook Time: **20** Minutes

Total Time: **30** Minutes

INGREDIENTS

- 8-10 slices ham
- 1 tablespoon olive oil
- ½ red onion
- 2 eggs
- ¼ tsp salt
- 2 oz. parmesan cheese
- 1 garlic clove
- ¼ tsp dill

DIRECTIONS

1. In a bowl whisk eggs with salt and parmesan cheese
2. In a frying pan heat olive oil and pour egg mixture
3. Add remaining ingredients and mix well
4. When prosciutto and eggs are cooked remove from heat and serve

ONION FRITATTA

Serves: **2**

Prep Time: **10**   Minutes

Cook Time: **20**   Minutes

Total Time: **30**   Minutes

INGREDIENTS

- 1 tablespoon olive oil
- ½ red onion
- 2 eggs
- ¼ tsp salt
- 2 oz. cheddar cheese
- 1 garlic clove
- ¼ tsp dill

DIRECTIONS

1. In a bowl whisk eggs with salt and cheese
2. In a frying pan heat olive oil and pour egg mixture
3. Add remaining ingredients and mix well
4. Serve when ready

FRIED CHICKEN WITH ALMONDS

Serves: **2**

Prep Time: **10** Minutes

Cook Time: **25** Minutes

Total Time: **35** Minutes

INGREDIENTS

- 1 cup bread crumbs
- ¼ cup parmesan cheese
- ¼ cup almonds
- 1 tsp salt
- 1 tablespoon parley leaves
- 1 clove garlic
- ½ cup olive oil
- 2 lb. chicken breast

DIRECTIONS

1. In a bowl combine parsley, almonds, garlic, parmesan, bread crumbs, salt and mix well
2. In a bowl add olive oil and dip chicken breast into olive oil
3. Place chicken into the breadcrumb mixture and toss to coat
4. Bake chicken at 375 F for 20-25 minutes
5. When ready remove chicken from the oven and serve

FILET MIGNON WITH TOMATO SAUCE

Serves: **4**

Prep Time: **10** Minutes

Cook Time: **30** Minutes

Total Time: **40** Minutes

INGREDIENTS

- 1 tsp soy sauce
- 1 tsp mustard
- 1 tsp parsley leaves
- 1 clove garlic
- 2-3 tomatoes
- 2 tsp olive oil
- 4-5 beef tenderloin steaks
- ½ tsp salt

DIRECTIONS

1. In a bowl combine parsley, garlic, soy sauce, mustard and mix well
2. Stir in tomatoes slices and toss to coat
3. In a skillet heat olive oil and place the steak
4. Cook until golden brown for 3-4 minutes
5. Transfer skillet to the oven and bake at 375 F for 8-10 minutes
6. When ready remove and serve with tomato sauce

ZUCCHINI NOODLES

Serves: *1*
Prep Time: *5*   Minutes

Cook Time: *15*   Minutes

Total Time: *20*   Minutes

INGREDIENTS

- 2 zucchinis
- 1 tablespoon olive oil
- 1 garlic clove
- ½ cup parmesan cheese
- 1 tsp salt

DIRECTIONS

1. Spiralize zucchini and set aside
2. In a skillet melt butter, add garlic and zucchini noodles
3. Toss to coat and cook for 5-6 minutes
4. When ready remove from the skillet and serve with parmesan cheese on top

GREEN BEANS WITH TOMATOES

Serves: **4**

Prep Time: **10**   Minutes

Cook Time: **15**   Minutes

Total Time: **25**   Minutes

INGREDIENTS

- 1 cup water
- 1 lb. green beans
- 2 tomatoes
- 1 tsp olive oil
- 1 tsp Italian dressing
- salt

DIRECTIONS

1. In a pot bring water to a boil
2. Add green beans, tomatoes and boil for 10-12 minutes
3. Remove green beans and tomatoes to a bowl
4. Chop tomatoes, add Italian dressing, olive oil and serve

ROASTED CAULIFLOWER RICE

Serves: **2**

Prep Time: **10**   Minutes

Cook Time: **25**   Minutes

Total Time: **35**   Minutes

INGREDIENTS

- 3-4 cups frozen cauliflower rice
- 1 tablespoon olive oil
- 2 garlic cloves
- ½ cup parmesan cheese

DIRECTIONS

1. Place the cauliflower rice on a sheet pan
2. Sprinkle garlic and olive oil over the cauliflower rice and toss well
3. Spread cauliflower rice in a single layer in the pan
4. Roast cauliflower rice at 375 F for 20-25 minutes
5. When ready remove from the oven and serve with parmesan cheese on top

ROASTED SQUASH

Serves: **3-4**

Prep Time: **10**   Minutes

Cook Time: **20**   Minutes

Total Time: **30**   Minutes

INGREDIENTS

- 2 delicata squashes
- 2 tablespoons olive oil
- 1 tsp curry powder
- 1 tsp salt

DIRECTIONS

1. Preheat the oven to 400 F
2. Cut everything in half lengthwise
3. Toss everything with olive oil and place onto a prepared baking sheet
4. Roast for 18-20 minutes at 400 F or until golden brown
5. When ready remove from the oven and serve

BRUSSELS SPROUT CHIPS

Serves: *2*
Prep Time: *10*   Minutes
Cook Time: *20*   Minutes
Total Time: *30*   Minutes

INGREDIENTS

- 1 lb. brussels sprouts
- 1 tablespoon olive oil
- 1 tablespoon parmesan cheese
- 1 tsp garlic powder
- 1 tsp seasoning

DIRECTIONS

1. Preheat the oven to 425 F
2. In a bowl toss everything with olive oil and seasoning
3. Spread everything onto a prepared baking sheet
4. Bake for 8-10 minutes or until crisp
5. When ready remove from the oven and serve

SQUASH CHIPS

Serves: **2**

Prep Time: **10**   Minutes

Cook Time: **20**   Minutes

Total Time: **30**   Minutes

INGREDIENTS

- 1 lb. squash
- 1 tablespoon olive oil
- 1 tsp garlic powder
- 1 tsp seasoning

DIRECTIONS

1. Preheat the oven to 425 F
2. In a bowl toss everything with olive oil and seasoning
3. Spread everything onto a prepared baking sheet
4. Bake for 8-10 minutes or until crisp
5. When ready remove from the oven and serve

ZUCCHINI CHIPS

Serves: **2**
Prep Time: **10**   Minutes

Cook Time: **20**   Minutes

Total Time: **30**   Minutes

INGREDIENTS

- 1 lb. zucchini
- 1 tablespoon olive oil
- 1 tablespoon parmesan cheese
- 1 tsp garlic powder
- 1 tsp seasoning

DIRECTIONS

1. Preheat the oven to 425 F
2. In a bowl toss everything with olive oil and seasoning
3. Spread everything onto a prepared baking sheet
4. Bake for 8-10 minutes or until crisp
5. When ready remove from the oven and serve

CARROT CHIPS

Serves: **2**

Prep Time: **10**   Minutes

Cook Time: **20**   Minutes

Total Time: **30**   Minutes

INGREDIENTS

- 1 lb. carrot
- 1 tablespoon olive oil
- 1 tablespoon parmesan cheese
- 1 tsp garlic powder
- 1 tsp seasoning

DIRECTIONS

1. Preheat the oven to 425 F
2. In a bowl toss everything with olive oil and seasoning
3. Spread everything onto a prepared baking sheet
4. Bake for 8-10 minutes or until crisp
5. When ready remove from the oven and serve

PASTA

SIMPLE SPAGHETTI

Serves: 2

Prep Time: 5   Minutes

Cook Time: 15   Minutes

Total Time: 20   Minutes

INGREDIENTS

- 10 oz. spaghetti
- 2 eggs
- ½ cup parmesan cheese
- 1 tsp black pepper
- Olive oil
- 1 tsp parsley
- 2 cloves garlic

DIRECTIONS

1. In a pot boil spaghetti (or any other type of pasta), drain and set aside
2. In a bowl whish eggs with parmesan cheese
3. In a skillet heat olive oil, add garlic and cook for 1-2 minutes
4. Pour egg mixture and mix well
5. Add pasta and stir well

6. When ready garnish with parsley and serve

ARTICHOKE PASTA

Serves: *2*
Prep Time: *5*   Minutes

Cook Time: *15*   Minutes

Total Time: *20*   Minutes

INGREDIENTS

- ¼ cup olive oil
- 1 jar artichokes
- 2 cloves garlic
- 1 tablespoon thyme leaves
- 1 lb. pasta
- 2 tablespoons butter
- 1. Cup basil
- ½ cup parmesan cheese

DIRECTIONS

1. In a pot boil spaghetti (or any other type of pasta), drain and set aside
2. Place all the ingredients for the sauce in a pot and bring to a simmer
3. Add pasta and mix well
4. When ready garnish with parmesan cheese and serve

CHICKEN PASTA

Serves: **2**

Prep Time: **5**   Minutes

Cook Time: **15**   Minutes

Total Time: **20**   Minutes

INGREDIENTS

- 1 lb. cooked chicken breast
- 8 oz. pasta
- 2 tablespoons butter
- 1 tablespoon garlic
- 1 tablespoon flour
- ½ cup milk
- ½ cup heavy cream
- 1 jar red bell peppers
- 2 tablespoons basil

DIRECTIONS

1. In a pot boil spaghetti (or any other type of pasta), drain and set aside
2. Place all the ingredients for the sauce in a pot and bring to a simmer
3. Add pasta and mix well
4. When ready garnish with parmesan cheese and serve

MEDITERRANEAN TUNA SALAD

Serves: **4**
Prep Time: **10** Minutes

Cook Time: **30** Minutes

Total Time: **40** Minutes

INGREDIENTS

- 2 cans tuna
- 2 celery stalks
- 1 cucumber
- 4 radishes
- 2 onions
- 1 red onion
- ¼ Kalamata olives
- 1 bunch parsley
- 10 mint leaves
- 1 tomato
- 1 serving mustard vinaigrette

DIRECTIONS

1. In a bowl combine all ingredients together
2. Add salad dressing and serve

MEXICAN TUNA SALAD

Serves: **2**

Prep Time: **5**   Minutes

Cook Time: **5**   Minutes

Total Time: **10**   Minutes

INGREDIENTS

- 2 cans tuna
- 1 red bell pepper
- 1 can black beans
- 1 can black olives
- 1 can yellow corn
- 2 tomatoes
- 2 avocados

DRESSING

- ½ cup Greek yogurt
- ¼ cup mayonnaise
- 1 tsp garlic powder
- ¼ tsp cumin

DIRECTIONS

1. In a bowl combine all ingredients together
2. In another bowl combine all ingredients for the dressing

3. Add dressing, mix well and serve

PRAWN NOODLE SALAD

Serves: **4**

Prep Time: **10**   Minutes

Cook Time: **10**   Minutes

Total Time: **20**   Minutes

INGREDIENTS

- ¼ lbs. noodle
- ¼ lbs. baby spinach
- 3 oz. cooked prawn
- ¼ lbs. snap pea
- 1 carrot

DRESSING

- 1 red chili
- 1 tsp fish sauce
- 1 tablespoon mint
- 2 tablespoons rice vinegar
- 1 tsp sugar

DIRECTIONS

1. In a bowl add all dressing ingredients and mix well
2. In another bowl add salad ingredients and mix well, pour dressing over salad and serve

ARUGULA AND SWEET POTATO SALAD

Serves: **2**

Prep Time: **10**   Minutes

Cook Time: **15**   Minutes

Total Time: **25**   Minutes

INGREDIENTS

- 1 lb. sweet potatoes
- 1 cup walnuts
- 1 tablespoon olive oil
- 1 cup water
- 1 tablespoon soy sauce
- 3 cups arugula

DIRECTIONS

1. Bake potatoes at 400 F until tender, remove and set aside
2. In a bowl drizzle, walnuts with olive oil and microwave for 2-3 minutes or until toasted
3. In a bowl combine all salad ingredients and mix well
4. Pour over soy sauce and serve

MANGO TANGO SALAD

Serves: **4**

Prep Time: **10**   Minutes

Cook Time: **30**   Minutes

Total Time: **40**   Minutes

INGREDIENTS

- 2 mangoes
- Juice of 1 lemon
- ¼ onion
- 1 tablespoon cilantro laves

DIRECTIONS

1. In a bowl combine all salad ingredients and mix well
2. Add salad dressing and serve when ready

COUSCOUS SALAD

Serves: *4*
Prep Time: *10*   Minutes

Cook Time: *30*   Minutes

Total Time: *40*   Minutes

INGREDIENTS

- 1 cup couscous
- 1 cup zucchini
- 1 red bell pepper
- ¼ cup red onion
- ¼ tsp cumin
- ¼ tsp black pepper
- ¼ cup salad dressing
- ¼ tsp parsley

DIRECTIONS

1. In a bowl combine all salad ingredients and mix well
2. Add salad dressing and serve when ready

NICOISE SALAD

Serves: **4**

Prep Time: **10** Minutes

Cook Time: **30** Minutes

Total Time: **40** Minutes

INGREDIENTS

- 1 oz. red potatoes
- 1 package green beans
- 2 eggs
- ½ cup tomatoes
- 2 tablespoons wine vinegar
- ¼ tsp salt
- ½ tsp pepper
- ½ tsp thyme
- ¼ cup olive oil
- 6 oz. tuna
- ¼ cup Kalamata olives

DIRECTIONS

1. In a bowl combine all ingredients together
2. Add salad dressing and serve

Serves: **2**
Prep Time: **10**   Minutes

Cook Time: **30**   Minutes

Total Time: **40**   Minutes

INGREDIENTS

- ¼ cup lemon juice
- ¼ cup rice wine vinegar
- 1 tsp sugar
- 1 cucumber
- ¼ cup mint
- 10 oz. cooked crab
- 2 cups mixed salad greens
- 2 lime wedges

DIRECTIONS

1. In a bowl combine all salad ingredients and mix well
2. Add salad dressing and serve when ready

FIFTH COOKBOOK

ZUCCHINI SOUP

Serves: **4**

Prep Time: **10**   Minutes

Cook Time: **20**   Minutes

Total Time: **30**   Minutes

INGREDIENTS

-   1 tablespoon olive oil
-   1 lb. zucchini
-   ¼ red onion
-   ½ cup all-purpose flour
-   ¼ tsp salt
-   ¼ tsp pepper
-   1 can vegetable broth
-   1 cup heavy cream

DIRECTIONS

1. In a saucepan heat olive oil and sauté zucchini until tender
2. Add remaining ingredients to the saucepan and bring to a boil
3. When all the vegetables are tender transfer to a blender and blend until smooth
4. Pour soup into bowls, garnish with parsley and serve

BROCOLI SOUP

Serves: **4**

Prep Time: **10**   Minutes

Cook Time: **20**   Minutes

Total Time: **30**   Minutes

INGREDIENTS

- 2 tablespoon olive oil
- 2 onons
- 2 garlic clvoes
- ¼ tsp red pepper flakes
- 2 lb. broccoli
- 1 potato

DIRECTIONS

1. In a saucepan heat olive oil and sauté brocoli until tender
2. Add remaining ingredients to the saucepan and bring to a boil
3. When all the vegetables are tender transfer to a blender and blend until smooth
4. Pour soup into bowls, garnish with parsley and serve

SIDE DISHES

FRIED VEGETABLES

Serves: **2**

Prep Time: **10** Minutes

Cook Time: **15** Minutes

Total Time: **25** Minutes

INGREDIENTS

- 1 cup red bell pepper
- ¼ cup cucumber
- ¼ cup zucchini
- ¼ cup asparagus
- ¼ cup carrots
- 1 onion
- 2 eggs
- 1 tsp salt
- 1 tsp pepper
- Seasoning
- 1 tablespoon olive oil

DIRECTIONS

1. In a skillet heat olive oil and sauté onion until soft
2. Chop vegetables into thin slices and pour over onion

3. Whisk eggs with salt and pepper and pour over the vegetables
4. Cook until vegetables are brown
5. When ready remove from heat and serve

ONION SAUCE

Serves: *4*

Prep Time: *10*   Minutes

Cook Time: *55*   Minutes

Total Time: *65*   Minutes

INGREDIENTS

- 1 onion
- 2 garlic cloves
- ¼ lb. carrots
- 1 potato
- 1 tablespoon balsamic vinegar
- ¼ tsp salt
- ¼ tsp black pepper
- 1 tablespoon olive oil
- 1 cup water

DIRECTIONS

1. Chop all the vegetables and place them in a heated skillet
2. Add remaining ingredients and cook on low heat
3. Allow to simmer for 40-45 minutes or until vegetables are soft
4. Transfer mixture to a blender and blend until smooth
5. When ready remove from the blender and serve

FISH "CAKE"

Serves: **4-6**

Prep Time: **10** Minutes

Cook Time: **50** Minutes

Total Time: **60** Minutes

INGREDIENTS

- 2 tuna tins
- 2 potatoes
- 2 eggs
- 1 handful of gluten free flour
- 1 handful of parsley
- black pepper
- 1 cup breadcrumbs

DIRECTIONS

1. Preheat the oven to 350 F
2. Boil the potatoes until they are soft
3. Mix the tuna with parsley, black pepper and salt
4. Roll fish into patties and dip into a bowl with flour, then eggs and then breadcrumbs
5. Place the patties on a baking tray
6. Bake at 350 F for 40-45 minutes
7. When ready remove from heat and serve

SUSHI HANDROLLS

Serves: **2**

Prep Time: **10**   Minutes

Cook Time: **25**   Minutes

Total Time: **35**   Minutes

INGREDIENTS

- 1 sushi nori packet
- 4 tablespoons mayonnaise
- ½ lb. smoked salmon
- 1 tsp wasabi
- 1 cup cooked sushi rice
- 1 avocado

DIRECTIONS

1. Cut avocado and into thin slices
2. Take a sheet of sushi and spread mayonnaise onto the sheet
3. Add rice, salmon and avocado
4. Roll and dip sushi into wasabi and serve

STEAMED VEGETABLES

Serves: *2*

Prep Time: *10*   Minutes

Cook Time: *10*   Minutes

Total Time: *20*   Minutes

INGREDIENTS

- 1 carrot
- 2 sweet potato
- 2 parsnips
- 1 zucchini
- 2 broccoli stems

DIRECTIONS

1. Chop vegetables into thin slices
2. Place all the vegetables into a steamer
3. Add enough water and cook on high until vegetables are steamed
4. When ready remove from the steamer and serve

GUACAMOLE

Serves: **2**

Prep Time: **5**   Minutes

Cook Time: **5**   Minutes

Total Time: **10**   Minutes

INGREDIENTS

- 1 avocado
- 1 lime juice
- 1 handful of coriander
- 1 tsp olive oil
- 1 tsp salt
- 1 tsp pepper

DIRECTIONS

1. Place all the ingredients in a blender
2. Blend until smooth and transfer to a bowl

CHICKEN NACHOS

Serves: **4-6**

Prep Time: **15**   Minutes

Cook Time: **35**   Minutes

Total Time: **50**   Minutes

INGREDIENTS

- 2 chicken breasts
- Tortilla chips
- Fajita seasoning
- ¼ cup cheddar cheese
- 4-5 mushrooms
- Guacamole
- ¼ cup peppers

DIRECTIONS

1. In a pan heat olive oil and add chopped onion, sauté until soft
2. Add chicken, fajita seasoning and remaining vegetables
3. Cook on low heat for 10-12 minutes
4. Place tortilla chips into a baking dish, sprinkle cheese and bake in the oven until cheese has melted
5. Remove from the oven pour sautéed vegetables and chicken over and tortilla chips and serve

SCRAMBLED EGGS WITH SALMON

Serves: **2**

Prep Time: **10** Minutes

Cook Time: **20** Minutes

Total Time: **30** Minutes

INGREDIENTS

- ½ lb. smoked salmon
- 2 eggs
- 1 avocado
- 1 tsp salt
- 1 tsp pepper
- 1 tps olive oil

DIRECTIONS

1. In a bowl whisk the eggs with salt and pepper
2. In a skillet heat olive oil and pour the egg mixture
3. Add salmon pieces to the mixture and cook for 2-3 minutes per side
4. When ready remove from the skillet, add avocado and serve

CHICKEN WITH RICE

Serves: *4*

Prep Time: *10* Minutes

Cook Time: *25* Minutes

Total Time: *35* Minutes

INGREDIENTS

- 2 chicken breasts
- 1 cup cooked white rice
- 2 tablespoons mayonnaise
- 1 tablespoon curry powder
- 1 zucchini
- 1 cup broccoli
- 1 tablespoon olive oil

DIRECTIONS

1. Cut chicken breast into small pieces and set aside
2. In a pan heat olive oil and cook the chicken breast for 4-5 minutes
3. In another bowl combine mayonnaise, curry powder and add mixture to the chicken
4. Add remaining ingredients and cook for another 10-12 minutes or until the chicken is ready
5. When ready remove from the pot and serve with white rice

ROASTED VEGETABLES

Serves: **2**

Prep Time: **10**   Minutes

Cook Time: **50**   Minutes

Total Time: **60**   Minutes

INGREDIENTS

- 1 carrot
- 2 sweet potatoes
- 1 butternut squash
- 2 parsnips
- 1 rosemary spring
- 2 bay leaves

DIRECTIONS

1. Chop the vegetables into thin slices
2. Place everything in a prepare baking dish
3. Bake at 350 F for 40-45 minutes or until vegetables are golden brown
4. When ready remove from the oven and serve

SLAW

Serves: *1*

Prep Time: 5   Minutes

Cook Time: 5   Minutes

Total Time: *10*   Minutes

INGREDIENTS

- 1 cabbage
- 1 bunch of baby carrots
- ½ cucumber
- 1 bun of cilantro
- 1 bunch of basil
- 1 onion

DIRECTIONS

1. In a bowl mix all ingredients and mix well
2. Serve with dressing

SRIRACHA DRESSING

Serves: *1*

Prep Time: 5   Minutes

Cook Time: 5   Minutes

Total Time: *10*   Minutes

INGREDIENTS

- 1 egg
- ¼ cup rice vinegar
- 1 tablespoon coconut aminos
- 1 tablespoon sriracha
- 1 tablespoon maple syrup

DIRECTIONS

1. In a bowl mix all ingredients and mix well
2. Serve with dressing

ARUGULA SALAD

Serves: *1*
Prep Time: 5   Minutes

Cook Time: 5   Minutes

Total Time: *10*   Minutes

INGREDIENTS

- 2 cups arugula leaves
- ¼ cup cranberries
- ¼ cup honey
- ¼ cup pecans
- 1 cup salad dressing

DIRECTIONS

1. In a bowl mix all ingredients and mix well
2. Serve with dressing

MASOOR SALAD

Serves: *1*
Prep Time: *5*   Minutes

Cook Time: *5*   Minutes

Total Time: *10*   Minutes

INGREDIENTS

- ¼ cup masoor
- ¼ cup cucumber
- ½ cup carrot
- ¼ cup tomatoes
- ¼ cup onion

SALAD DRESSING

- ¼ tablespoon olive oil
- 1 tsp lemon juice
- ¼ tsp green chillies
- ½ tsp black pepper

DIRECTIONS

1. In a bowl combine all ingredients together
2. Add salad dressing, toss well and serve

MUSKMELON AND PEAR SALAD

Serves: *1*
Prep Time: *5*   Minutes

Cook Time: *5*   Minutes

Total Time: *10* Minutes

INGREDIENTS

- 1 cup muskmelon
- ½ cup pear cubes
- ½ cup apple cubes
- Salad dressing

DIRECTIONS

1. In a bowl combine all ingredients together
2. Add salad dressing, toss well and serve

CITRUS WATERMELON SALAD

Serves: **1**

Prep Time: **5**   Minutes

Cook Time: **5**   Minutes

Total Time: **10**   Minutes

INGREDIENTS

- 2 cups watermelon
- ¼ cup orange
- ¼ cup sweet lime
- ¼ cup pomegranate

SALAD DRESSING

- 1 tsp olive oil
- 1 tsp lemon juice
- 1 tablespoon parsley

DIRECTIONS

1. In a bowl combine all ingredients together
2. Add salad dressing, toss well and serve

POTATO SALAD

Serves: 2

Prep Time: 5   Minutes

Cook Time: 10   Minutes

Total Time: 15   Minutes

INGREDIENTS

- 5 potatoes
- 1 tsp cumin seeds
- 1/3 cup oil
- 2 tsp mustard
- 1 red onion
- 2 cloves garlic
- 1/3 cup lemon juice
- 1 tsp sea salt

DIRECTIONS

1. Steam the potatoes until tender
2. Mix mustard, turmeric powder, lemon juice, cumin seeds, and salt
3. Place the potatoes in a bowl and pour the lemon mixture over
4. Add the chopped onion and minced garlic over
5. Stir to coat and refrigerate covered
6. Add oil and stir before serving

CARROT SALAD

Serves: 2

Prep Time: 5   Minutes

Cook Time: 5   Minutes

Total Time: *10*   Minutes

INGREDIENTS

- 1 ½ tbs lemon juice
- 1/3 tsp salt
- ¼ tsp black pepper
- 2 tbs olive oil
- 1/3 lb carrots
- 1 tsp mustard

DIRECTIONS

1. Mix mustard, lemon juice and oil together
2. Peel and shred the carrots in a bowl
3. Stir in the dressing and season with salt and pepper
4. Mix well and allow to chill for at least 30 minutes

MOROCCAN SALAD

Serves: **2**

Prep Time: **5** Minutes

Cook Time: **5** Minutes

Total Time: **10** Minutes

INGREDIENTS

- 2 tbs lemon juice
- 1 tsp cumin
- 1 tsp paprika
- 3 tbs olive oil
- 2 cloves garlic
- 5 carrots
- Salt
- Pepper

DIRECTIONS

1. Peel and slice the carrots
2. Add the carrots in boiled water and simmer for at least 5 minutes
3. Drain and rinse the carrots under cold water
4. Add in a bowl
5. Mix the lemon juice, garlic, cumin, paprika, and olive oil together

6. Pour the mixture over the carrots and toss then season with salt and pepper
7. Serve immediately

AVOCADO CHICKEN SALAD

Serves: 2

Prep Time: 5   Minutes

Cook Time: 5   Minutes

Total Time: 10 Minutes

INGREDIENTS

- 3 tsp lime juice
- 3 tbs cilantro
- 1 chicken breast
- 1 avocado
- 1/3 cup onion
- 1 apple
- 1 cup celery
- Salt
- Pepper
- Olive oil

DIRECTIONS

1. Dice the chicken breast
2. Season with salt and pepper and cook into a greased skillet until golden
3. Dice the vegetables and place over the chicken in a bowl
4. Mash the avocado and sprinkle in the cilantro

5. Season with salt and pepper and add lime juice
6. Serve drizzled with olive oil

ASPARAGUS FRITATTA

Serves: *2*
Prep Time: *10*   Minutes

Cook Time: *20*   Minutes

Total Time: *30*   Minutes

INGREDIENTS

- ½ lb. asparagus
- 1 tablespoon olive oil
- ½ red onion
- ¼ tsp salt
- 2 oz. cheddar cheese
- 1 garlic clove
- ¼ tsp dill

DIRECTIONS

1. In a bowl whisk eggs with salt and cheese
2. In a frying pan heat olive oil and pour egg mixture
3. Add remaining ingredients and mix well
4. Serve when ready

EGGPLANT FRITATTA

Serves: **2**

Prep Time: **10**   Minutes

Cook Time: **20**   Minutes

Total Time: **30**   Minutes

INGREDIENTS

- ½ lb. eggplant
- 1 tablespoon olive oil
- ½ red onion
- ¼ tsp salt
- 2 oz. cheddar cheese
- 1 garlic clove
- ¼ tsp dill

DIRECTIONS

1. In a bowl whisk eggs with salt and cheese
2. In a frying pan heat olive oil and pour egg mixture
3. Add remaining ingredients and mix well
4. Serve when ready

KALE FRITATTA

Serves: **2**

Prep Time: **10** Minutes

Cook Time: **20** Minutes

Total Time: **30** Minutes

INGREDIENTS

- ½ lb. kale
- 1 tablespoon olive oil
- ½ red onion
- ¼ tsp salt
- 2 oz. parmesan cheese
- 1 garlic clove
- ¼ tsp dill

DIRECTIONS

1. In a bowl whisk eggs with salt and parmesan cheese
2. In a frying pan heat olive oil and pour egg mixture
3. Add remaining ingredients and mix well
4. Serve when ready

BROCCOLI FRITATTA

Serves: **2**

Prep Time: **10**   Minutes

Cook Time: **20**   Minutes

Total Time: **30**   Minutes

INGREDIENTS

- 1 cup broccoli
- 1 tablespoon olive oil
- ½ red onion
- ¼ tsp salt
- 2 oz. cheddar cheese
- 1 garlic clove
- ¼ tsp dill

DIRECTIONS

1. In a skillet sauté broccoli until tender
2. In a bowl whisk eggs with salt and cheese
3. In a frying pan heat olive oil and pour egg mixture
4. Add remaining ingredients and mix well
5. When ready serve with sautéed broccoli

STUFFED SWEET POTATOES

Serves: **4**

Prep Time: **10** Minutes

Cook Time: **20** Minutes

Total Time: **30** Minutes

INGREDIENTS

- 2 lbs sweet potatoes
- 1 avocado
- 1/3 cup cilantro
- 1 jalapeno
- 2 tbs olive oil
- 1 cup black beans
- 1 red onion
- 2 garlic cloves
- 1 cup corn
- 1 cup tomatoes
- 2 tbs taco seasoning
- ½ tsp salt

DIRECTIONS

1. Cook the sweet potatoes as you desire
2. Sauté the jalapeno and red onion in olive oil for 3 minutes

3. Add minced garlic and cook for 1 more minute
4. Add the black beans, corn, seasoning, salt, and pepper and cook 5 more minutes
5. Scoop out the potato insides and fill with the mixture
6. Serve with sour cream

CHICKEN AND RICE

Serves: **4**

Prep Time: **10** Minutes

Cook Time: **20** Minutes

Total Time: **30** Minutes

INGREDIENTS

- 1 cup rice
- 3 tsp seasoning
- 4 chicken breasts
- 2 ½ tbs butter
- 2 ½ cup chicken broth
- 1 lemon
- Salt
- Pepper

DIRECTIONS

1. Season the chicken with salt, pepper and seasoning
2. Cook in melted butter until golden on both sides
3. Add in chicken broth, rice, lemon juice and remaining seasoning
4. Cook covered for at least 20 minutes

LIVER AND MASHED VEGETABLES

Serves: **4**

Prep Time: **20**   Minutes

Cook Time: **40**   Minutes

Total Time: **60**   Minutes

INGREDIENTS

- 3 tsp rapeseed oil
- 350g sweet potato
- 150g parsnip
- 320g green beans
- 350g swede
- 3 cloves garlic
- 15 g flour
- 4 onions
- 1 pack liver
- 1 cube lamb stock
- Black pepper

DIRECTIONS

1. Cook the onions in hot oil for about 20 minutes
2. Coat the liver with flour and pepper and cook in a pan until brown
3. Add the garlic to the onions and stir in 2 tsp of flour

4. Dissolve the stock cube in 450 ml water, then pour over the onions and bring to a boil
5. Add the liver and cook for 5 more minutes
6. Boil the vegetables covered for about 15 minutes
7. Mash the potato, parsnip and swede together
8. Serve the liver with the mashed vegetables

BROCCOLI CASSEROLE

Serves: **4**

Prep Time: **10**   Minutes

Cook Time: **15**   Minutes

Total Time: **25**   Minutes

INGREDIENTS

- 1 onion
- 2 chicken breasts
- 2 tablespoons unsalted butter
- 2 eggs
- 2 cups cooked rice
- 2 cups cheese
- 1 cup parmesan cheese
- 2 cups cooked broccoli

DIRECTIONS

1. Sauté the veggies and set aside
2. Preheat the oven to 425 F
3. Transfer the sautéed veggies to a baking dish, add remaining ingredients to the baking dish
4. Mix well, add seasoning and place the dish in the oven
5. Bake for 12-15 minutes or until slightly brown
6. When ready remove from the oven and serve

ROASTED SQUASH

Serves: **3-4**

Prep Time: **10**   Minutes

Cook Time: **20**   Minutes

Total Time: **30**   Minutes

INGREDIENTS

- 2 delicata squashes
- 2 tablespoons olive oil
- 1 tsp curry powder
- 1 tsp salt

DIRECTIONS

1. Preheat the oven to 400 F
2. Cut everything in half lengthwise
3. Toss everything with olive oil and place onto a prepared baking sheet
4. Roast for 18-20 minutes at 400 F or until golden brown
5. When ready remove from the oven and serve

ZUCCHINI CHIPS

Serves: **2**

Prep Time: **10**   Minutes

Cook Time: **20**   Minutes

Total Time: **30**   Minutes

INGREDIENTS

- 1 lb. zucchini
- 1 tablespoon salt
- 1 tsp smoked paprika

DIRECTIONS

1. Preheat the oven to 425 F
2. In a bowl toss everything with olive oil and seasoning
3. Spread everything onto a prepared baking sheet
4. Bake for 8-10 minutes or until crisp
5. When ready remove from the oven and serve

POTATO CHIPS

Serves: *2*

Prep Time: *10* Minutes

Cook Time: *20* Minutes

Total Time: *30* Minutes

INGREDIENTS

- 1 lb. zucchini
- 1 tablespoon salt
- 1 tsp smoked paprika

DIRECTIONS

1. Preheat the oven to 425 F
2. In a bowl toss everything with olive oil and seasoning
3. Spread everything onto a prepared baking sheet
4. Bake for 8-10 minutes or until crisp
5. When ready remove from the oven and serve

PIZZA

ZUCCHINI PIZZA

Serves: **6-8**
Prep Time: **10**   Minutes

Cook Time: **15**   Minutes

Total Time: **25**   Minutes

INGREDIENTS

- 1 pizza crust
- ½ cup tomato sauce
- ¼ black pepper
- 1 cup zucchini slices
- 1 cup mozzarella cheese
- 1 cup olives

DIRECTIONS

1. Spread tomato sauce on the pizza crust
2. Place all the toppings on the pizza crust
3. Bake the pizza at 425 F for 12-15 minutes
4. When ready remove pizza from the oven and serve

RICOTTA PIZZA

Serves: **6-8**
Prep Time: **10**   Minutes

Cook Time: **15**   Minutes

Total Time: **25**   Minutes

INGREDIENTS

- 1 pizza crust
- 8 oz. ricotta cheese
- 1 clove garlic
- 2 oz. parmesan cheese
- ½ lb. baby leaf greens
- 1 tablespoon olive oil

DIRECTIONS

1. Spread tomato sauce on the pizza crust
2. Place all the toppings on the pizza crust
3. Bake the pizza at 425 F for 12-15 minutes
4. When ready remove pizza from the oven and serve

SALMON PIZZA

Serves: *6-8*
Prep Time: *10*   Minutes

Cook Time: *15*   Minutes

Total Time: *25*   Minutes

INGREDIENTS

- 1 pizza crust
- 1 shallot
- 1 parmesan cheese
- ½ red onion
- 2 tablespoons olive oil
- ½ lb. smoked salmon
- ½ lemon

DIRECTIONS

1. Spread tomato sauce on the pizza crust
2. Place all the toppings on the pizza crust
3. Bake the pizza at 425 F for 12-15 minutes
4. When ready remove pizza from the oven and serve

GREEN OLIVE PIZZA

Serves: **6-8**

Prep Time: **10** Minutes

Cook Time: **15** Minutes

Total Time: **25** Minutes

INGREDIENTS

- 1 onion
- 1 pizza crust
- 1 cup green olives
- 1 clove garlic
- ½ lb. potatoes
- ½ lb. taleggio

DIRECTIONS

1. Spread tomato sauce on the pizza crust
2. Place all the toppings on the pizza crust
3. Bake the pizza at 425 F for 12-15 minutes
4. When ready remove pizza from the oven and serve

CAULIFLOWER PIZZA

Serves: *6-8*
Prep Time: *10*   Minutes

Cook Time: *15*   Minutes

Total Time: *25*   Minutes

INGREDIENTS

- 1 pizza crust
- 2 oz. parmesan cheese
- 1 tablespoon olive oil
- 4-5 basil leaves
- 1 cup mozzarella cheese
- 1 cup cauliflower

DIRECTIONS

1. Spread tomato sauce on the pizza crust
2. Place all the toppings on the pizza crust
3. Bake the pizza at 425 F for 12-15 minutes
4. When ready remove pizza from the oven and serve

ARTICHOKE AND SPINACH PIZZA

Serves: *6-8*
Prep Time: *10*   Minutes

Cook Time: *15*   Minutes

Total Time: *25*   Minutes

INGREDIENTS

- 1 pizza crust
- 1 garlic clove
- ½ lb. spinach
- ½ lb. soft cheese
- 2 oz. artichoke hearts
- 1 cup mozzarella cheese
- 1 tablespoon olive oil

DIRECTIONS

1. Spread tomato sauce on the pizza crust
2. Place all the toppings on the pizza crust
3. Bake the pizza at 425 F for 12-15 minutes
4. When ready remove pizza from the oven and serve

MINT PIZZA

Serves: **6-8**
Prep Time: **10**   Minutes

Cook Time: **15**   Minutes

Total Time: **25**   Minutes

INGREDIENTS

- 1 pizza crust
- 1 olive oil
- 1 garlic clove
- 1 cup mozzarella cheese
- 2 oz. mint
- 2 courgettes

DIRECTIONS

1. Spread tomato sauce on the pizza crust
2. Place all the toppings on the pizza crust
3. Bake the pizza at 425 F for 12-15 minutes
4. When ready remove pizza from the oven and serve

SAUSAGE PIZZA

Serves: **6-8**
Prep Time: **10**   Minutes

Cook Time: **15**   Minutes

Total Time: **25**   Minutes

INGREDIENTS

- 2 pork sausages
- 1 tablespoon olive oil
- 2 garlic cloves
- 1 tsp fennel seeds
- ½ lb. ricotta
- 1 cup mozzarella cheese
- 1 oz. parmesan cheese
- 1 pizza crust

DIRECTIONS

1. Spread tomato sauce on the pizza crust
2. Place all the toppings on the pizza crust
3. Bake the pizza at 425 F for 12-15 minutes
4. When ready remove pizza from the oven and serve

HEALTY PIZZA

Serves: **6-8**

Prep Time: **10** Minutes

Cook Time: **15** Minutes

Total Time: **25** Minutes

INGREDIENTS

- 1 pizza crust
- 1 tablespoon olive oil
- 1 garlic clove
- 1 cup tomatoes
- 1 cup mozzarella cheese
- 1 carrot
- 1 cucumber

DIRECTIONS

1. Spread tomato sauce on the pizza crust
2. Place all the toppings on the pizza crust
3. Bake the pizza at 425 F for 12-15 minutes
4. When ready remove pizza from the oven and serve